You can't get THERE from HERE

Part 1

Demystifying the Internet so you can be the
Master of your online Universe

ISBN: 978-0-6151-7933-9

www.youcantgetthere.com

Text, Illustrations & Songs by Carissa Vivirito

For Nils
Endless bike trails and chest-high powder

The scanning, uploading, and distribution of this book via the Internet or via any other means without the permission of the author or publisher is illegal and punishable by crushing. Side effects may include nausea and vomiting. Pregnant women should not handle this book, as it is known to cause incidences of excessive hair growth. Void where prohibited.

Doodle and note-taking space

Doodle and note-taking space

Contents

Doodle and note-taking space

Foreword

Dear Reader,

I've never met Carissa Vivirito. In fact, it's a given that I would spend more time on hold with the cable company than the time she and I have conversed thus far. Perhaps like you, I got to know Carissa through this book. Carissa emailed *"You Can't Get THERE From HERE"* unsolicited. I liked the title, I liked her, and I liked this book.

Carissa's goal " is to blast through this barrier of mysterious unknowns using common language and humor." Mission accomplished!

Any expert can impress readers with 10-dollar words and lots of acronyms that only other near-experts would even bother to decode. But it takes real understanding, humility, and generous respect for the reader to be willing and able to simplify complex ideas without condescending.

I've written three books. Two were Wall Street Journal and New York Times bestsellers. Still, I wish I had written one like this.

If you're HERE, and want to know how to get THERE, read this book!

Sincerely,

Jeffrey Eisenberg, Co-Founder & CEO of Future Now Inc.
Co-Author of #1 best-selling Wall Street Journal, New York Times, USA Today and BusinessWeek best sellers *"Call To Action: Secret Formulas for Improving Online Results"* and *"Waiting For Your Cat To Bark? Persuading Customers When They Ignore Marketing"*

Doodle and note-taking space

Introduction

I promise that the majority of this book will be a unique combination of education and humor, so please bare with me (anybody catch that one? Please bare "get naked" with me) while I set the stage initially with some rather dull background on the Internet and its related professional practices. If you already know all this and want to get right into the fun reading, turn to page 12.

History of the Internet *(Cue 2001: A Space Odyssey Title Music)*

The Internet as a communication concept has been in existence since the 1960s, though the widely available commercial World Wide Web as we know it today, was born in the 1990s with the advent of Graphical User Interface (GUIs) browsers like Mosaic, Netscape and Internet Explorer.

The Internet picked up impressive steam in 1995 (the year I graduated from high school), when its expansion into people's homes and adoption by legitimate services and organizations proved its validity. It was around this time that the World Wide Web Consortium (often referred to as the W3C **w3.org**) was formed, the "governmental" body of the online community, established to set standards for universal functionality across the Web.

Five years into this exciting growth pattern where millions were made and thrown at .com projects, the proverbial "Dot-Com" bubble burst in 2000, triggering massive lay-offs, financial losses and a general attitude of fear and doubt toward the Internet's potential.

Although the Internet has steadily rebuilt much of this lost confidence over the last 7 years, the Internet is still very much a market in its infancy. And though nearly 70% of the U.S. is online regularly, checking email, shopping online or viewing the latest You Tube hilarities, in my nearly 10 years in the industry, I continually run into the same fear-based and doubtful attitudes spurned by the 2000 bust.

With nearly 100 Million registered domain names (*www.yourname.com*) in the U.S. at the time of this writing, the media's near constant focus on online threats to safety, identity or worse, and a surprising lack of education programs explaining what the Internet is really about, it's no wonder people are fearful.

Goal of this Book

The goal of this book is to blast through this barrier of mysterious unknowns using common language and humor. It is my vision that this book provides insight into the big bad world of the Internet and leaves you feeling empowered to tackle whatever Internet project comes your way. So roll up your sleeves and let's kick some Internet ass!

To garner more truly delightful, edge-of-your-seat action about the history of the Internet, visit **livinginternet.com**, and **internet101.org** for overview information and **internetworldstats.com** for detailed usage statistics by country.

My Perspective

Though this book is not about me specifically, I have written it in a very personal and conversational style. I will often weave in personal anecdotes and the analogies I present to explain Internet concepts were born out of my nearly 10 years of professional experience within the industry.

Half of these years were spent in the practice area of **Information Architecture**. I realize that this is not a practice area such as business law, or pediatrics, which you likely have some familiarity with and can relate to. Therefore, I will give a brief overview of what information architecture is.

The Information Architecture Institute (**iainstitute.org**) defines it as:

1. The structural design of shared information environments.
2. The art and science of organizing and labeling web sites, intranets, online communities and software to support usability.
3. An emerging community of practice focused on bringing principles of design and architecture to the digital landscape.

I define it more simply as the organization, labeling and flow of Web sites. It's much like the role an architect plays in designing a building and its systems, only for a Web site.

The Internet from 10,000 Feet (safe for all portable electronics)

To ensure you have enough baseline understanding of the Internet from the perspective that I will be discussing it, here is what it looks like from high above:

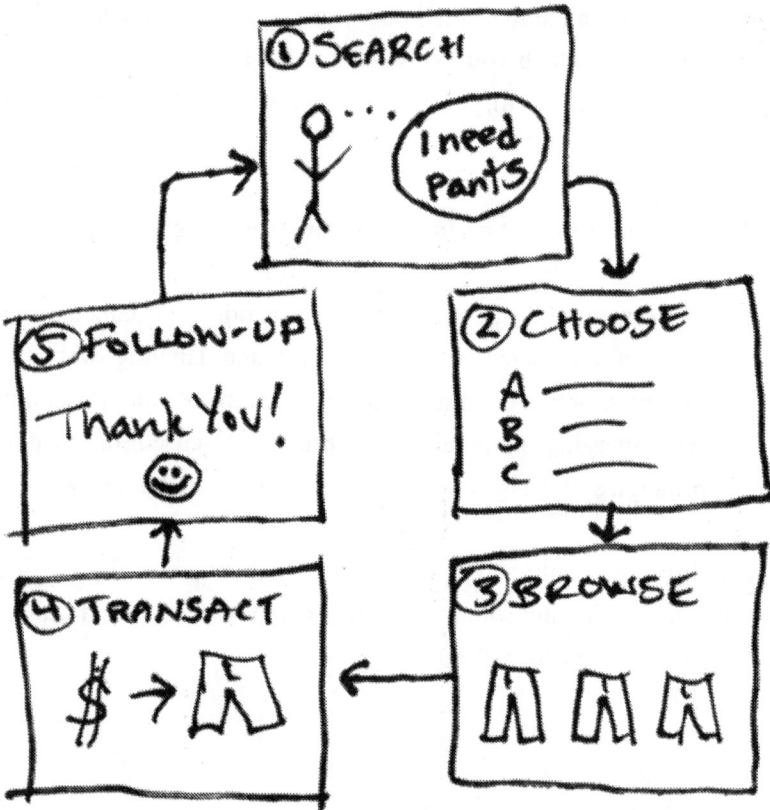

1. I need some new pants so I **search** using Google
2. I view the matching results and make my **choice**
3. I **browse** the Web site and find what I am looking for
4. I enter credit information and **purchase** my new pants
5. I receive a **follow-up** confirmation email and am happy!

This example is overly simplistic and focuses on ecommerce. However, the general concepts of **seeking** something online, be it a product, service or social networking site (myspace, facebook, youtube, etc.), **choosing** where to go based on visual and textual clues, **browsing** a site for what you are looking for, completing your session by **fulfilling a task** (purchase, fill out form, download information) and a **follow-up** on that action, can be applied to most Internet experiences.

One distinction I would like to make at this point is that even when there is no obvious follow-up for you as a user, such as a confirmation email or follow-up communication, there is a hidden follow-up behind the scenes of the Web site in terms of tracking what you do, or don't do; and using that data to refine how a Web site is put together.

The key to mastering the Internet is the understanding of how important all of these elements are to achieving your intended goals. All steps must be considered in a successful online strategy. Omitting one or more can spell disaster, or, at a minimum, the inability to best leverage your Web site as a business tool.

It's all very Gestalt (the whole of which is greater than the sum of its parts)!

This book is for you if you….

- Ever have, currently are, or plan on working in one of the following areas:
    - o   Web Site Design & Development
    - o   Marketing / Online Marketing
    - o   Inside / Outside Sales within any industry
    - o   Company, Service or Product Management
    - o   Own your own company
    - o   Unemployed (let's face it, you've got the time)

- Wonder why everyone seems to do everything the same way, even when it makes no sense and you want to force your fist through a wall when this happens

- Have a degree of humor; concentration in sarcasm

- Are a self-proclaimed expert on everything, as this will add to your repertoire, though I am sure you already know everything I have to go over in this book, so on second thought, maybe you shouldn't read this book since you are so frigging smart

- Like me, music, neither, or both

Tips and notes for reading further

🖱 Anywhere you see this icon, it means the text has an accompanying video and song viewable online to further comprehension and enjoyment of the topic at hand. Original songs (unless noted otherwise) accompanying the book include:

- o "Three is A Magic Number" – Children/Folk (Blind Melon / School House Rocks)
- o "In the Eyes of a Search Engine" – Pop Country
- o "You Can't Get There from Here" – Folk

🖱 I will attempt to reference sources of inspiration where applicable throughout the text, but understand that I am of the belief that most things have been done already and I would be sadly mistaken to think I have the ability to recall the origination of every spark or idea I have ever had. This also applies to those who may question my originality or proclaim they already thought of or saw this or that, well good for you and them because I'm too lazy to search that much.

🖱 Yes, I purposely chose the ultra-cheesy computer mouse bullets

🖱 All drawings in this book were done on the back of Dilbert daily calendar comics in an effort to save the environment. If this book does really well and I become super famous from that or posthumously, I will sell the original drawings for hundreds of thousands of dollars – let me know if you're interested!

🖱 I may, on occasion, feel the need to sprinkle mild profanity into the text to enhance your experience or mine

🖱 I would like to note that I attempt to create and execute all things in my life (this book included) through a lens of

Love, laughter and greatness of spirit

So if anything contained herein seems mean-spirited, offensive or [insert your own word] I can assure you that you are taking yourself and your life far too seriously, lighten up!

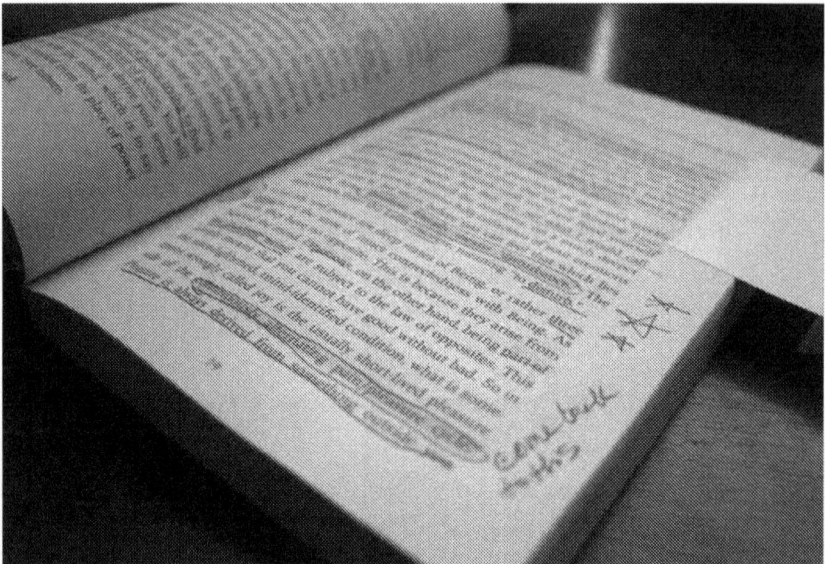

Sample of how I devour & mark-up books when I read, feel free to do the same to this one!

How this book came to be

I awoke at 3:16am the morning of Tuesday August 21, 2007. Instead of the typical reason for awaking at such an hour (a bladder-full of wine), my brain was flooded with flurries (is it okay to combine different weather metaphors like that?) of quirky and seemingly comical analogies for Internet-industry practices.

While this may seem nerdy, I have always dreamed about my line of work, and although I have argued that this time should in fact be billable, it has never panned out in my favor. Until now of course, as this book stands to be my shining representation that dreaming "on the clock" can in fact generate oodles of revenue (case in point: you bought this book).

But let me back up, 19 hours previous to the awakening (pun intended), for the first and last time in my life, I no longer worked for another company. Holymotherflippinsugartits this is the best feeling I have ever felt, the excitement and anticipation of the final few clicks of the climbing roller coaster combined with the butterflies in my belly from the weightless swoosh down.

There is no malice intended to my former workplaces, but as any fumbling entrepreneur knows, it's our internal struggle between jumping and safety that brew an unbelievable amount of resentment, that, unless properly focused, can cause massive destruction. My sincerest apologies go out to the many who have suffered my wrath from such.

The point in this step back in time is to explain the newfound freedom my brain was spouting as if on crack (note: I have never tried crack).

The proverbial floodgates had been burst. Time to crank (I haven't tried crank either).

After letting these ingenious Web-world analogies tumble around my tired brain for a bit, combined with the natural anchor tug to fall back asleep, a voice boomed out: "Life rewards action, get out of bed you slacker!

With this subliminal command, I raced to the computer and in a matter of minutes had outlined the full series of chapters you now read. You could say this book is my own version of the golden tablets handed to Joseph Smith from the Angel Moroni (I am not Mormon, but know many and mean no offense as it is simply a comparison that looped nicely with a plug for where I grew up and allowed me to offer props to my Dad), which is fitting since I grew up a stone's throw away from Palmyra, NY and my father taught at the Palmyra/ Macedon high school for 20 years.

I like to think of this smack of inspiration more like the trick my Dad used to play on me where he would put one hand out and say, "Look at this" while smacking me upside the back of my head with a, "but watch out for that."

Thanks Dad. Your girl's dun ya proud.

—

Doodle and note-taking space

About Me

I have no delusions of grandeur about my relative anonymity, and I do not profess anything in this book to be right, true, amazing or even useful to all that read it. With this said, I have left my unabridged story for the end of the book, since most of you could care less about who I am. If you are that interested, turn to the back and be amazed! Ooooh….ahhhh…

Sparks of Genius

I always get little nuggets of wisdom stuck in my teeth with every book I read (refer to image on page 14). It may be presumptuous of me to think you will get so from this book, but should the mood strike you, please feel free to **highlight**, **underline**, **doodle**, **remark** or correct anything you read. I have afforded ample white space in the margins, front, back and page breaks that should allow for such. I will also reference sites, books, and other materials; a full index of which is provided at the back.

And There's More…

You thought you were just getting a book out of this deal? Nosireebob, there's **even more fun-filled content online** including a blog and videos. I will be writing additional content from time to time on the blog and would love to feature your comments as well.

If you are so inclined to share your thoughts and ideas from the book, are looking for infamous credit in a later work of mine, or simply want to keep the conversation going, please visit the exclusive readers' book site at **youcantgetthere.com/iamhere** to contribute to the blog and watch the videos.

1 The Milk's in the Back

I begin the analogies with the one that was screaming out to me loudest from my sleep on that fateful Tuesday morning, and so we go…

I am constantly intrigued by how different the world of online commerce is from traditional brick and mortar. Here is a chart demonstrating a few examples of what I mean:

Traditional Store	Online Store
Milk is all the way in the back by the beer to ensure you buy way more crap than you need or want	Whatever you are looking for better be right under your nose or you're out of there
You never know what your total order amount will be until checkout at the register, where you and your guests are cleverly distracted by tabloids and trinkets	You know at every single second of your shopping experience just how many items and how much money you are shelling out, making it that much easier to come to your senses and abandon ship (or cart, as it were) – this would be like putting a scanner and running total in your offline cart!
The fun sugar-packed cereal, toys and candy are at kid eye-level, ripe for chubby little hands to grab, beg and plead for mommy to buy	Everything is very categorized and compartmentalized. Let's say I am browsing the clearance clothing at Target.com and right next to this pops up some awesome Spongebob candy or Dora the Explorer sneakers, again, I'd be gone….

You get the idea, and can probably come up with a lot more examples of this inverse phenomenon. My **challenge to the online community** is to more synergistically merge the time-tested buying psychology of traditional stores with the online world. I know I would spend a lot more! And we all know how much marketing people get behind anything that involves "synergistic" concepts.

Just imagine if your online conversion rate (typical ranges are **2%-4%**, *Fireclick Index*) rivaled traditional brick and mortar successful conversion rates of **48%** *(Underhill, "Call to Action", Eisenberg)*. That would add up to some serious profit margin!

To see how your Web site stacks up to industry standards for conversion rates, visits, cart abandonment rates and other key metrics, fireclick has assembled live analytics as shown on the next page. It's always great to know how you are performing in comparison to the norm, but even better is being able to **compare your data against itself** month over month and year over year.

One traditional shopping experience example I can recall does, in fact, bring a bit of the online world to the real world of squeaky-wheeled crooked carts. I recall a time when grocery stores and a few other big box retailers placed calculators on the cart handles. Perhaps I was too young to utilize its true value, but all I ever did was enter 1134 or 8008 (spells "HELL" and "BOOB" when looked at upside down) into the calculator to piss off my Mom. The point I am making is that by pounding people over the head with the fact we are spending money just takes all the fun out of the shopping experience, so get rid of it, or at least test it out!

Fireclick
A DIGITAL RIVER COMPANY

Top Line Growth | Fashion and Apparel | Electronics | Catalog | Specialty | Outdoor and Sports | Software

Fireclick, an industry leading provider of web analytics services, is proud to introduce the world's first publicly-available web analytics benchmark index. The Fireclick Index provides an objective comparison of key metrics across a variety of segments. Compare the performance of your online business to the many successful industry leading web sites using Fireclick today!

Top Line Growth

Business Metrics	This Week	Last Week	% Change
Conversion Rate: Global	2.30%	2.30%	0%
Conversion Rate: First Time Visitors	2.20%	2.30%	-4% ▼
Conversion Rate: Repeat Visitors	2.30%	2.40%	-4% ▼
Cart Abandonment Rate	71.90%	71.60%	0%

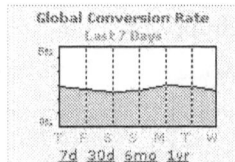

Marketing Metrics	This Week	Last Week	% Change
Conversion Rate: Keywords	3.50%	3.40%	3% ▲
Conversion Rate: Emails	3.10%	3.20%	-3% ▼
Conversion Rate: Affiliates	1.70%	1.80%	-6% ▼

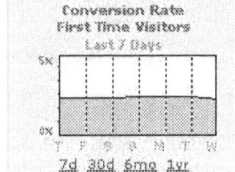

Site Metrics	This Week	Last Week	% Change
Average Session Length (pages)	6.00	6.10	-2% ▼
Average Session Duration (min)	3.40	3.50	-3% ▼
Average Page Display Time (s)	3.90	3.90	0%
Average Page Read Time (s)	24.60	24.70	0%
Average Connection Speed (Kbps)	155.50	162.90	-5% ▼

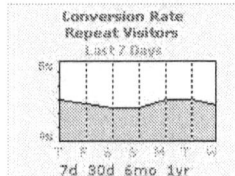

Global Conversion Rate
Last 7 Days
7d 30d 6mo 1yr

Conversion Rate
First Time Visitors
Last 7 Days
7d 30d 6mo 1yr

Conversion Rate
Repeat Visitors
Last 7 Days
7d 30d 6mo 1yr

index.fireclick.com

I think the use of entertaining distraction is something that could be tried out online. I mention earlier the candy, rag mags and other fun things at checkout aisles. I also know that when waiting in long lines at Disney World, they purposely put up mirrors and video screens, because they know we **Americans just can't get enough of ourselves**, or TV. Clever technique to make you forget you are sweating in 90 degree sunshine next to screaming kiddies with $10-Mickey-Mouse-ice-cream-bar-stained-cheeks.

What if when you clicked to checkout online you got to watch some hilarious video or listen to something fun? I don't know if it would work, but it's worth a try!

And finally, I can personally attest that the best ingredient for increased online Average Order Value (AOV) I have found is **drinking and shopping**. I can't count how many times I have arrived home from work to find multiple packages at my doorstep. Oooh, what a fun surprise! Who sent me a package? As I proceed to open the packages, I quickly realize I have been the victim once again of the late night online drunken e-commerce pillage. At least I am still cheap and frugal even when buzzed so I don't suffer the charges later. I bring up this amusing story to suggest that perhaps we should run user tests on e-commerce sites with individuals sober and then inebriated to see if they spend more; a new sort of comparative testing. I'd sign up!

2 Where do you keep the spoons?

Have you ever been at a friend's or relative's house and reached to grab a spoon from the most logical place in the kitchen only to be unpleasantly surprised by sandwich bags and aluminum foil, the "junk" drawer, or a hand gun (this has happened to me on more than one occasion, but it could have something to do with living in a pro-gun state like Arizona)?

So you try another drawer. Nope. Now you are on a hot pursuit, opening and closing drawers, feeling annoyed, frustrated and stupid. Your friend calls out, "What are you looking for?" and so as not to appear the token dumb ass you state, "Nothing, I'll find it," when whew, just in time the FINAL drawer reveals the silverware.

Why is it that other people don't put things where they belong? Why isn't everyone exactly like you? As awesome as you can imagine that world to be, most people's mental organization schema is as unique as their body odor (I thought of using the similes 'snowflake' or 'fingerprint', but they seemed so tired and lame).

This silverware drawer example is a perfect analogy for how site visitors hunt and peck to find what they are looking for online. You can begin to imagine how many possible scenarios must be considered when designing for such. It's pretty overwhelming at first, but there are a lot of useful resources and experts (learn how to find one on pages 64-66) out there to help you out. I will list these at the back of the book if you care.

The spoon analogy can extend to an entire kitchen. I like to use this example to get people engaged with how to construct logical, user-centric site architectures (also called site maps, blueprints, site organization, box and arrow drawing thingies). Let's take a shot, trust me it will be super duper fun! You can even play along if you have some paper and crayons.

This is an aerial view of my kitchen:

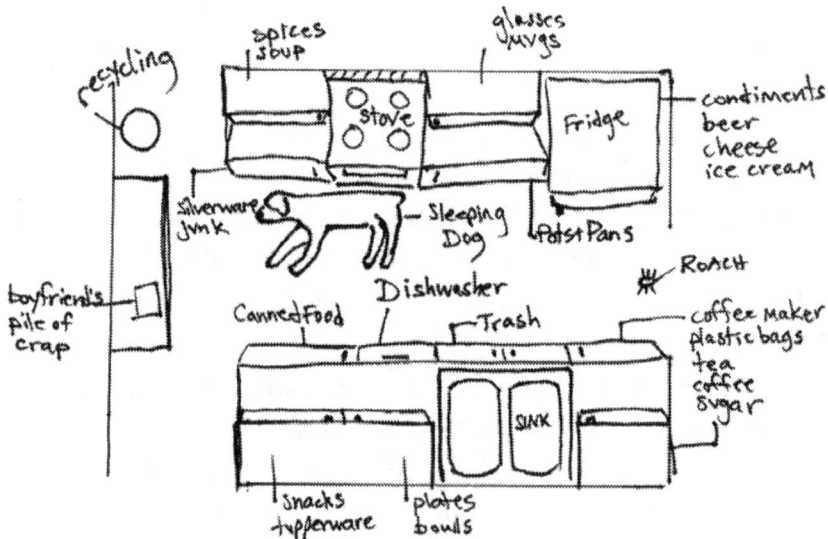

I have outlined all the high-level appliances, cabinets and containers, as well as the top level of items kept within each. **A direct relationship can be drawn between this physical organization and a conceptual site map for a Web site.** Here is how some terms correlate between the two:

Kitchen Drawing	>	Site Map
Main Categories	>	Meta Data
Large Item Names	>	Primary Navigation
Small Item Names	>	Secondary Navigation

Labels of Things	>	Taxonomy
Individual Items	>	Content
Sleeping Dog	>	Annoying Pop-ups
Roach	>	404 Error Page

This is what a Web site map of my kitchen could look like:

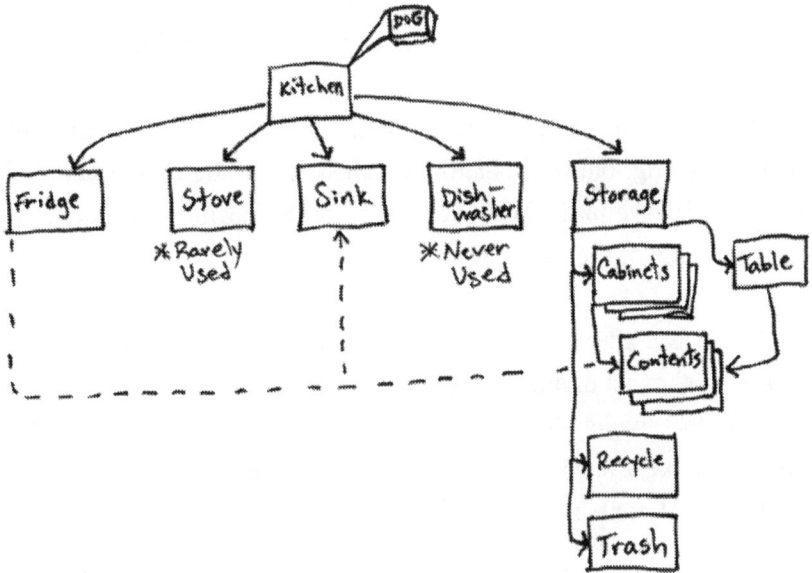

I have indicated the kitchen as the "HOME" page, the appliances and storage apparatus as the primary navigation and drawn relationships between the content shared by multiple containers (dotted lines). In the world of Information Architecture (the practice of making these site map thingies) we would qualify a site map like this as rather broad and not very deep, except in the "Storage" section. We could also say that this Web site has potential for a Content Management System (CMS) since the dotted lines and stacks of boxes/pages (multiple occurrences of similar or like items such as cabinets and contents) indicate shared content.

You can also observe that I ordered my primary navigation items from **left to right in order of my mental model of importance**. I deem the fridge the most important, since I use it the most, the stove next since I use it less (the dog really does lay in front of it constantly so I can't even get to it), but more than the sink and dishwasher (my boyfriend does all the dishes, but he also dirties most of them, lucky me!).

And I bet you would have created a very different site map from my kitchen drawing, but more than likely there would be some overlap. It is this overlap we in the Web world aim for, to ideally cover the habits of the majority of the online population.

Let's pour us a glass of wine, put our feet up and stay in the kitchen to discuss another set of analogous systems. Here is a peek into one of my cabinets, that which holds drinking containers. The cabinet in this example is like a page of a Web site, the items within, a representation of the types of content one may find on that page:

My thinking in my organization of the drinking container cabinet, since I am only 5'4", is that I place the most frequently used items on the bottom, least used on top. A Web page would be the opposite: **most frequently used / important items on top,** more detail on the bottom.

Plus, my boyfriend is taller (5'11") and he uses the travel mugs & beer coozies most (is it pronounced kozy or koozy? I just had an intense debate with my aunt and cousins about this, I say it is koozy, because who the hell wants to drink a beer out of a kozy; those are the things country folk knit to put on their toasters and tissue boxes because they are completely out of touch with reality).

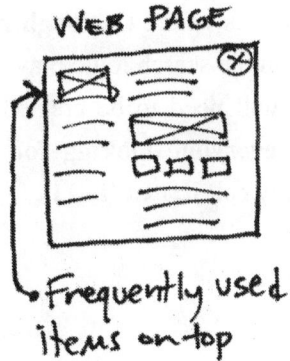

He just picked up this beer coozie in Alabama that on one side reads, "Don't Sweat the Petty Things" and on the other side, "Don't Pet the Sweaty Things." I guess that's the type of wisdom they have to offer in Alabama. Way to go south!

And now we have another opportunity to correlate the kitchen to the wondrous world of Web:

Shelf Levels	>	Hierarchy
Labels of Items	>	Taxonomy
Placement by User	>	Usability
Beer Coozie Wisdom	>	Engaging Content

One final point, and then I will put the kitchen analogy to rest for now. Take note of the labels I gave the items in my cabinet: travel mugs, plastic cups, beer coozies, coffee mugs, drinking glasses. Not all people would call these items the same things that I do. You may call drinking glasses "grown-up cups" if you have kids or if you are still a kid at heart. This is where **thorough research into labeling conventions**, as well as online search logic play key roles in your plan. The database for the site will need to be created to allow for this level of detail. This ensures **everyone looking for you and your offerings, no matter what they call it, can find it.**

Now go eat!

3 The Rule of Threes

*Visit **youcantgetthere.com/iamhere** for "Three is A Magic Number"*

We have all either heard or said some version of one of the following:

> *"If it takes more than three clicks, I'm outta' there"*

> *"Users need to be able to get to anything on the site within 3 clicks"*

Or how about this one:

> *"There should never be more than 7 main navigation items"*

Both the concept of threes and the rule of sevens have some great basis in other theories. You may be familiar with George Miller's (1956) study on short-term memory recall surrounding the number seven. This study is commonly associated with explanations for seven digit phone numbers. And no, I am not that smart, I checked this out on Wikipedia for verification.

I recall the rule of 3-clicks being a frequent request of clients beginning around the year 2000. I never quite understood the obsession with this, especially at the 11th hour of testing when the CEO steps in to "play around with the site a bit" and insists that this or that page absolutely MUST be reachable within 3 clicks because he read it in a magazine on a plane and the whole site needs to be redesigned.

I didn't completely invalidate either of these rules as a starting point for the general public or business world, heck, any attention paid to the importance of the Web as a business tool that early in the game was a win. However, I would remind everyone that these "rules" came out of the very early set of standards developed prior to any deep repetitive testing or analysis. I have read many articles debunking both of these myths, but in either case, here is what I have garnered over my years of crafting site architectures and online strategies.

Three

In addition to being one of the coolest prime numbers ever, I have a personal affinity for the number three. I won't let this cloud my Internet-specific tips on such, but I'd like to start there. Here are my observations on the number three:

3 points or lines are the minimum needed to create dimension

3 is the fundamental requirement for structure stabilization

US Government: Legislative, Judicial and Executive

Leverage: 3 points, fulcrum as center

The Holy Trinity: Father, Son and Holy Ghost

Mind, Body and Spirit

Above, Below, Within

Think, Feel, Act

Be, Do, Have

Here, There, Neither Here nor There

Past, Present, Future

Before, Now, After

Birth, Life, Death

Overall, pretty cool to think about; how the number 3 provides the ultimate blend of form and function, balance and potential. Now I will venture from the abstract into the Internet and where the rules of 3 apply.

Navigation Structures

You may be familiar with the following labels for types of navigation:

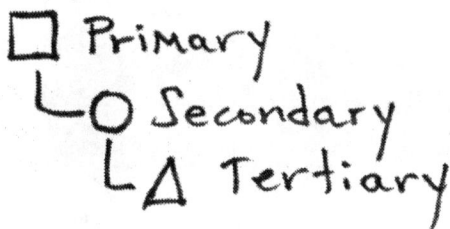

The **Primary** navigation is the top-level, typically running down the left-hand side of the page or across the top. **Secondary** is the next level down and **Tertiary** under the second level.

Less important than the rule of 3 clicks, is the rule of 3 levels of site navigation. Check out your own personal or company Web site. Does it suffer from navigation level overload? Does your site navigation structure look more like varicose veins than a nice organized outline? Any links below a third level should be handled as "**Contextual Links**". These are most often links within the site content, or copy. They could also be handled as a graphic button or promotion, but never, ever should you start adding Quaternary, Quintanary and a bunch of other nonexistent, made-up word levels of navigation. But hey, if you can prove me wrong, let me know!

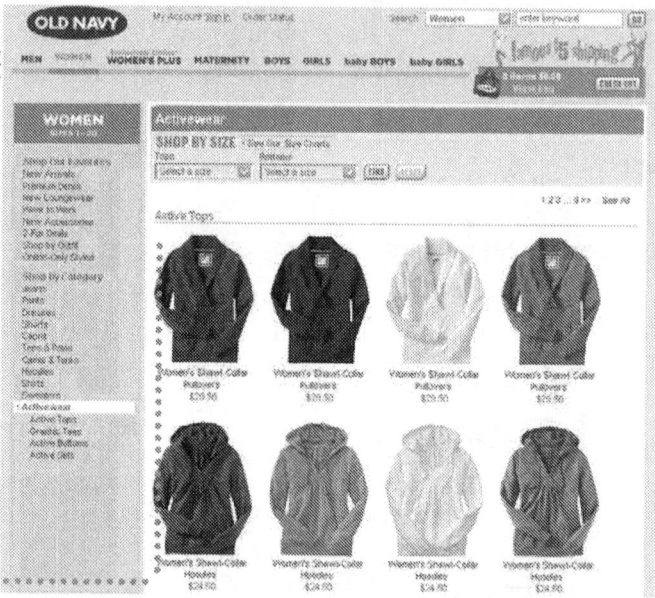

Primary

Secondary

Tertiary

Contextual
Links

oldnavy.com

There is no harm in trying to get people to where they want to be in as few clicks as possible, but foregoing good page layout or organization of content for this arbitrary rule is a no-no in my book.

Page Layouts

Keeping a rule of 3, or more specifically in this case, a triangle in mind, when designing pages is a very smart practice. Multiple eye-tracking studies have been conducted to observe where Internet users move their eyes, how long they linger in places and where they eventually click. You may have seen some of these studies; here are a few sample visuals:

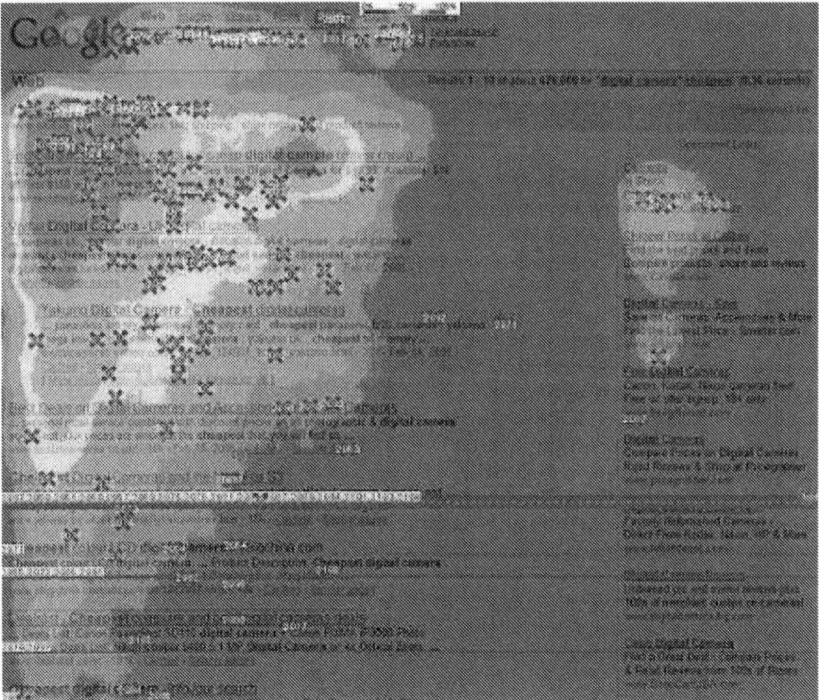

Did-It, Enquiro, and EyeTools: did-it.com, enquiroresearch.com, eyetools.com

Please note that if you are reading the print version, these charts are in black and white because color printing is ridiculously expensive and I would have had to charge you $45 for this book. Each of these diagrams is a "heat map" style image with the darkest gray in the upper right being red, the bands emanating from that point out following the Roy G Biv spectrum. To compensate, I have provided full color images of these, and any other difficult to decipher images on the companion reader Web site at **youcantgetthere.com/iamhere**

Websiteoptimization.com

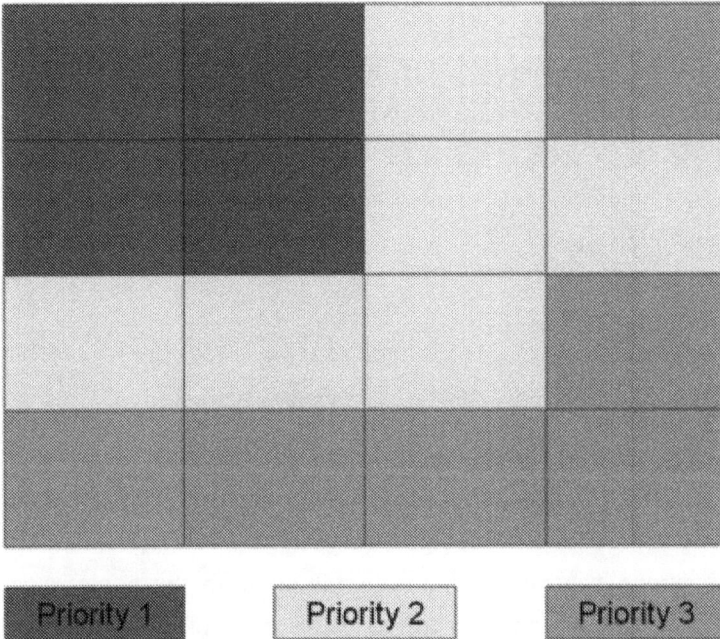

Eyetrack III: poynterextra.org

The prior 3 charts are samples of studies ranging from where users look on search engine page results to the importance of standardized navigation placement and finally, a great overall grid approach for importance of placement on the page.

The lesson here is: **give people what they expect**. Put the **most important message and call to action in the upper left and middle** of the page, less important items at the bottom and right. Seems simple enough, but you would be amazed how much room for improvement there is.

Navigation Numbers

Okay, listen up, you listening? THERE IS NO RULE FOR SEVEN NAVIGATION ITEMS AND THE NEXT PERSON THAT INSISTS THIS TO ME IS GOING TO GET IT. Now that that's out of the way, let me provide you some tips on how to know what number of items is right for your Web site.

Tip #1: Chunking

This shouldn't be a new concept. We've been doing it since we were babies, making piles of like things. All the circles go here, the squares there and the other junk over there. The same concept that works for infants works for adults as well, big surprise! Now don't take what I am saying the wrong way and link to everything from the home page. There are limits to how far you can take this concept, but lets take a look at some sites that have far more than 7 primary navigation items, but by employing successful chunking techniques, make it work.

The red Envelope site uses **chunking** in its Secondary navigation to organize over 25 separate links. You can see how the information is easier to digest and doesn't require users to "hunt and peck" for what they're looking for.

Sample Chunking Headers ....

*re∂*ENVELOPE

occasion	recipient	shops

occasion
think pink
anniversary
new baby
birthday
good luck
just because
wedding
see more>

recipient
for her
for him
for baby
for mother
for father
for teacher
see more >

shops
what's new
jewelry
men's accessories
home + garden
think pink
bar + wine + cigars
flowers + plants
personalized gifts
sale shop
see more >

Why are yo

favorites –

redenvelope.com

Many Web sites don't even need 7 navigation items. You may be able to craft a successful strategy with 3 or 4 items, especially if you are a small business or simply need to provide basic information. Chunking typically applies to larger, more complex sites, but there is definitely a tipping point. If, even after chunking, the primary navigation grows outside the arena of 40-50 items, you may be a perfect case for multiple-audience or experience-level Web sites.

Tip #2: Hierarchy

Similar to chunking, hierarchy is another method to employ when approaching navigation schemas. Both practices take a relatively complex set of items and simplify them by **grouping them into larger buckets** (chunking) or applying **visual cues to assist the user** in digesting the information (hierarchy).

Much of hierarchy can find its roots in Information Design. This specialty is exactly what it sounds like, taking complex information, be it text, image, voice, data, statistics, and designing it in a way that anyone can understand. One of the most distinguished experts in this area is Edward Tufte. He is masterful at visual communication of complex information. Check out his work at **edwardtufte.com**.

My Information Design Professor, Chris Paccione (one of the amazing and talented founders of Body Media, a company dedicated to health awareness via wearable body monitoring devices **bodymedia.com**) introduced me to one of my favorite designs of complex information.

He presented the class an amazing visual display in one of Edward Tufte's books. Charles Joseph Minard's visual depiction of Napoleon's March in the War of 1812 is a spectacular example of well-crafted information design. The top bar shows the losses going into Moscow, the bottom black the retreat, all exquisitely tied to time and temperature, brilliant! Get one for yourself: **edwardtufte.com/tufte/ posters.**

Napoleon's March to Moscow, The War of 1812, Charles Joseph Minard:

Hierarchy can be thought of much like a woman presents herself for a night on the town. Let's say her primary objective is to attract a nice young man for a night of bump and grind on the dance floor. She knows her best asset are her eyes, so she plays them up with her make-up and wears a bright blue sparkly blouse to match them.

Once she attracts men with her bewitching gaze, she entraps them with her super fly dance moves, so she is sure to wear some nice hot pants to allow maximum gyration.

Finally, if the guy is a great dancer, she will carry on some light conversation on a smoke break outside, revealing to him her scathingly sharp intellect.

In the woman's mind her hierarchy for successful attraction is as follows: Eyes > Legs > Bump and Grind > Intellect. Throwing all of this girl power at a guy at once (lacking hierarchy) would be overwhelming and scare off most.

Following are some great samples of hierarchy in navigation and layout design online. See if you can distinguish how each design attracts your eye to the most important information, while also allowing multiple levels of deeper information within the section.

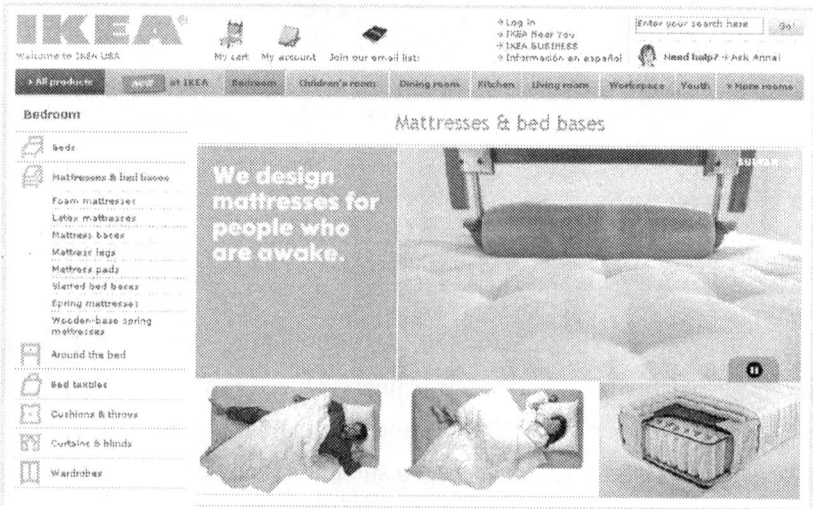

ikea.com/us

- What is the primary message or image (try letting your eyes go out of focus)?

- What do you notice first, second and third? If it helps, go ahead and label the top 3 items in order of importance visually. How do you think this may correlate to the objectives of the Web site and goals of the business?

- What questions are in your mind as you view this page and where would you click next?

redenvelope.com

◦ What is the primary message or image (try letting your eyes go out of focus)?

◦ What do you notice first, second and third? If it helps, go ahead and label the top 3 items in order of importance visually. How do you think this may correlate to the objectives of the Web site and goals of the business?

◦ What questions are in your mind as you view this page and where would you click next?

cafepress.com

- What is the primary message or image (try letting your eyes go out of focus)?

- What do you notice first, second and third? If it helps, go ahead and label the top 3 items in order of importance visually. How do you think this may correlate to the objectives of the Web site and goals of the business?

- What questions are in your mind as you view this page and where would you click next?

yellowstonepark.org

◦ What is the primary message or image (try letting your eyes go out of focus)?

◦ What do you notice first, second and third? If it helps, go ahead and label the top 3 items in order of importance visually. How do you think this may correlate to the objectives of the Web site and goals of the business?

◦ What questions are in your mind as you view this page and where would you click next?

Tip #3: Testing and Tracking

The thing that always drove me nuts in the early days of designing navigations and structures for clients was never knowing if what I created was actually correct or completely pulled from my nether regions. Perhaps it's the OCD, math wizard, or wannabe quantum physicist in me that longs for correct answers that I can check, recheck and verify, but my early site maps and architectures were thrown up there to see what stuck. Luckily I have always had an uncanny knack to somehow magically create successful online structures even before we were able to test them as well as we can today. Yay me!

The days of complete guesswork are over, hip hip hooray! Now we have access to amazing tracking tools like Google Analytics (**google.com/analytics**), Omniture (**omniture.com**), Clicktracks (**clicktracks.com**) and many, many more. Google Analytics is all the tool most businesses will ever need, so give it a test run today, or contact a capable staffer or firm to assist you with your online metrics (to find a qualified firm, see page 64-66). For larger organizations with in-house Web teams, Omniture, Clicktracks or other enterprise level solutions should be considered.

It is not uncommon to not know what your Web site key metrics are, or should be, but in an age where the information is readily available, even FREE with Google Analytics, there really is no excuse not to. You may even have seen a report or logged into an analytics tool for your site, but for the life of you, couldn't make heads nor tails of all that data. The key to getting on top of your site metrics is to **pare down all that complex data to its simplest form** and give you the true business data you seek.

The following metrics, or key performance indicators (KPIs) are a starting point:

1. **Visits**: total visits over period of time (day, month, year) to observe trends. Note that this is NOT page views or hits, but unique visitors to the site.

2. **Conversion Rate**: total site conversions divided by total visits over period of time. For example, say you have 10,000 visits in one month and 250 purchases (or completed forms, however you define a conversion). Your conversion rate would be 2.5%. Refer to the Fireclick index (**index.fireclick.com**) presented in chapter 1 for comparative data on how your conversion rates stack up.

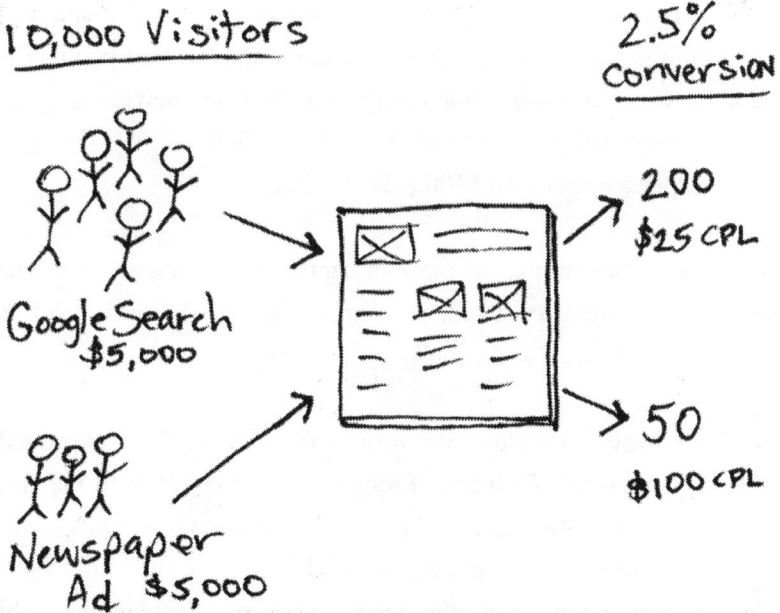

3. **Cost Per Lead**: total leads divided into total budget for time period. This can also be referred to as cost per sale or cost per acquisition, depending on your business model (service inquiry form as lead versus ecommerce purchase). So if those 250 purchases/leads for the month were the result of a monthly online marketing budget of $10,000, you paid $40 per lead. Once you have a good handle on this data, you can compare it to other marketing channels. The Web will more often than not provide the most cost effective rate, but be cautious about yanking dollars from elsewhere as successful marketing campaigns combine multifaceted approaches.

4. **Cost Per Lead by Referral Source**: cost per lead broken down by source. So if your monthly marketing budget of $10,000 is split 50/50 between online marketing and newspaper ads (sending users to a unique URL www.yourname.com/newspaper), but you receive 200 leads from online marketing and 50 from newspaper, your online cost per lead would be $25 ($5,000 / 200) and your newspaper cost per lead $100 ($5000 / 50).

This is just the beginning; for more in depth information about metrics and ways to improve on them, pick up a copy of Bryan and Jeffrey Eisenberg's book "Call to Action".

Also **never underestimate the importance of a fully standards compliant and valid Web site**. From the first keystroke to the final database plug, always validate your code to ensure compatibility with a wide range of browsers (Explorer, Safari, Firefox), accessibility levels (hearing-impaired, etc.), and other readers such as search engines. This process in essence checks your code against the proper and accepted grammar of the Web. Access these tools at **validator.w3.org.**

So after all of your labors on organizing and reorganizing your Web site architecture, navigation and flow, you can test and track your theories and tweak your site over time based on user feedback. This is, of course, if you were savvy enough to develop the site structure in a means that is easily editable, and you actually installed accurate tracking correctly from the beginning.

It's always something!

Visit **youcantgetthere.com/iamhere** *for "Three is A Magic Number"*

Three is the magic number: Complete Lyrics

Three, oh, it's the magic number,
Yeah it is, it's the magic number

Somewhere in that ancient mystic trinity
You get three
It's the magic number

With the past and the present and the future
And faith and hope and charity
And the heart and the brain and the body
It'll give you three; it's a magic number,

It takes three legs to make a tripod
Or to make a table stand
And it takes three wheels to make a vehicle
And call it a tricycle
Every triangle has three corners
Every triangle has three sides

No more, no less
You don't have to guess
That is three, can't you see?
It's the magic number

A man and a woman had a little baby
Yes they did,
There were three in the family
That's the magic number

3 6 9
12 15 18
21 24 27
30

Now multiply backwards from 3 x 10

Oh, well 3 x 10 is 30
And 3 x 9 is 27
3 x 8 is 24
3 x 7 is 21
3 x 6 is 18
3 x 5 is 15
3 x 4 is 12
And 3 x 3 is 9
And 3 x 2 is 6
And 3 x 1 is 3, of course

A man and a woman had a little baby
There were three in the family
And that's the magic number

4 A Second Opinion

Be pre-warned that this chapter is likely to include one or more rants, but all in the spirit of education.

I'm going to cover three angles on this topic:

1. The idea that for the most part, we don't question doctors
2. We do not have dedicated doctors, we are lucky if we see him / her once per year
3. When things are really serious, we are delusional, the doctor is incompetent, or we outright disagree, we get a 2nd opinion

1. We don't question our doctors

For the most part, when my Doctor tells me a diagnosis, treatment plan, or pretty much anything, I do what he says. Not because I am a compliant individual as anyone who knows me can tell you, I prefer to break every rule possible and question everything, or at the very minimum, learn the rules so well in order to win via the rules no one else knows. No. I do what he says because **he is the expert**. I don't have a degree in whatever he has a degree in. I don't know why my whatever is doing this or that and makes me feel such and such. He does (or at least I believe he is a lot closer than my analysis). He gets paid very well to be good at what he does. End of story.

Now, for the sake of argument, let's say I engage an Internet firm to redesign my Web site and online marketing initiatives for a one-time set-up cost of $75,000 and an ongoing annual budget of $150,000 (pretty close to a good doctor's salary).

I chose this firm because they have over 10 years of experience in the industry, my business peers recommended them, and the team on my project has worked on projects 10x smaller and larger than mine.

Everything is going great, I love the approach they recommend, the design is phenomenal, the customer service outstanding. They even explain things to me in a way I can understand and this begins to seem very logical, heck, I bet I could even create a site map.

I take another look at the site map and plan and now that I look at it again, I see a TON of things that make much more sense. In fact, why did they do it this way, I would never call our product that! What are they thinking! What? That's not what I want on our home page, our customers don't need to be asked questions, they need to know as much as they can about my company and what we do. We already know everything about our customers, so why should we waste any time or money asking them?

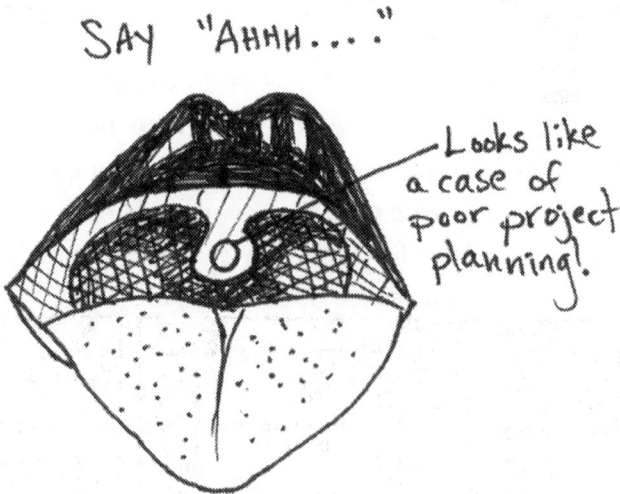

SAY "AHHH...."

Looks like a case of poor project planning!

In my 30 years running this place, we have never ever called our products anything other than what they have always been called, are these people morons? Why am I paying them so much? I need to call and get some answers…

And on and on and on…

If you haven't been on the giving or receiving end of one of these conversations, I am certain you can identify with it.

If you hire a company because they are experts at what they do, for the love of everything holy, please, please, please just let them be the expert. Do not question their expertise, recommendations or treat them like you would your landscaper. In fact, don't treat your landscaper like your landscaper. **Everyone deserves respect and dignity**.

Just like they tell you to be nice to your waiter or chef, at least until after the meal, because you know what they could do, I take a stand that we all treat our Internet professionals with the same respect. After all, they hold a key business tool in their hands. Let them work their magic. Or maybe we just all need to get Doctorates in Internet Strategy.

2. We don't have dedicated doctors

In most service professions, created to serve those seeking what they have to offer, there are tens, hundreds, thousands, sometimes even millions of customers. Just to name a few: doctors, lawyers, mechanics, masseurs, architects, landscapers, etc.

Why do we then, as a general rule, choose to remember this in some circumstances, but not in others? I envision a conversation similar to one I have been on the receiving end of countless times occurring with a Doctor (okay, play along, I know a Doctor would rarely take a call but his or her assistant would, so not all that different in most other professions) as such:

Patient (P): Hello Doctor, I don't understand why you can't see me today.

Doctor (D): Well, I am already booked solid and have filled all of my emergency case slots.

P: But I am paying you good money and my little pinky toe hurts, if you don't see me, I'll go elsewhere.

D: Now calm down, upon the initial inspection of your little pinky toe I found there to be a slight bruise that needs to be iced and given time to heal.

P: This is bullshit! Let me talk to your boss, this is completely unacceptable! No one talks to me this way!

D: Uhhhh, okay...[click]

You may think I am over-dramatizing for effect, but let me assure you I am not. I swear on my little pinky toe.

I wonder if the label of "Patient" gives more passivity to a person than calling them "Customer" or "Partner"? Maybe we as Web professionals should start calling our customers "Patients" or "Students" or maybe "Big Inconsiderate Jerk Wads"!

3. Get a second opinion

Okay, so to balance out the one-sidedness of this chapter, I will say that if you have truly lost faith in your selected Internet firm, go ahead and get a second opinion (see page 64 on how to find a firm). After all, opinions are like assholes, everyone has one and most of them stink.

5 You Can't Get There From Here

 *Visit **youcantgetthere.com/iamhere** for "You Can't Get There from Here"*

If you've never been lost in the sticks, pulled over to ask a local for directions, only to get back, "You can't git thar from here" in the applicable regional accent, you are truly missing out. Aside from the obvious impossibility of the statement, it's always fun to experience truly entertaining ignorance.

Perhaps one of the most tried and true analogies around, this colloquialism hints at the **simple genius of roadways as a means for understanding the Internet**.

My favorite way to begin this exercise is to imagine you are building the most exciting, desirable and fulfilling location you can. I'm going to make mine a combination casino / amusement park / beach, as so:

Notice the bar by the beach. This is essential, and there would be bar-boys (or girls for all you guys and lesbians out there) coming out to ensure you always have a full glass. I purposely didn't include a pool bar, because I think they are disgusting. Whose ingenious idea was it to stick a bunch of drunks with full bladders in a warm tub of water to hang out? I guess it's the true kiddie pool for grown-ups, but count me out. One time I dared to open my eyes under water at a kiddie pool and thought I would be blind forever.

You can make your dream location whatever you wish, just make sure it doesn't steal business from mine! Okay, now lets pretend this destination is in the middle of rural Kansas. Let's also pretend there are absolutely no roadways, signage, maps or people that know how to get there, like this:

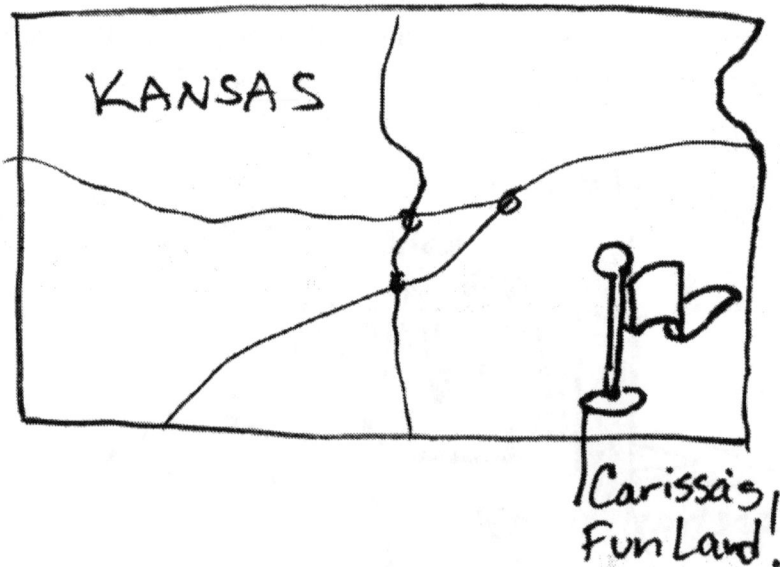

So it seems the only people who would come to my super fun casino / amusement park / beach are those with helicopters, horses or ATVs; and they would only be able to get there if I actually found a way to tell them about it (and if I built it with them in mind instead of me).

Okay, enough with the land of make believe. This may seem completely ridiculous, but so is investing $25,000, $75,000 or even $150,000 in building an amazing Web site with the best products, tools, resources, bells and whistles and then doing absolutely no planning or investing in the infrastructure or marketing.

I have seen this happen time and time again with clients, so the sooner you can start thinking like a real estate tycoon, the better your online strategy will be.

How do you know what you are building is right for the customer?

How will your ideal customer find you?

What routes will they take to get there and how will you track this?

Do the roads already exist or do you need to partner with others to build them?

Once they get there, how will they know where to go to get what they want?

The questions are endless, and most people are more familiar with physical concepts like buildings, maps and roads. This is a great way to engage all levels of people in meaningful discussions regarding their Web project. Give it a try and let me know how it goes!

And for some more practical advice about **how to build online roads that lead to your site**, we can look at the some of the ways to do so:

1. Search Engines
2. Media Buys
3. Social Media

1. Search Engines

More than 8 out of 10 online users begin their Internet sessions at a search engine, 5 of those 8 never look past the first page of results.

With nearly 233 Million people online in the U.S. (70% of the population), nearly 116 Million of them won't find you if you aren't listed on the first page of Google, Yahoo, MSN or Ask.com search results for relevant key words (**internetworldstats.com**).

Google and Yahoo, comprising more than **85%** of all search engine volume (**hitwise.com**), see a range between **60%-75%** (**enquiro.com**) of all clicks from organic listings versus paid.

Generally speaking, a **strong search engine strategy should include a balance of both** for the following reasons:

Organic Search: also called natural search or search engine optimization (SEO). Although there are no hard costs (ad spend) associated with this, there is still a service or resource cost for the expertise to be listed organically. The majority of clicks to your Web site will come from this type, but you can only be ranked well for a **limited set** of key terms or phrases (**3-7**) due to the formulas of how the search engines determine rankings. SEO also **takes time to see results**.

Paid Search: often referred to as Pay Per Click (PPC). Although PPC receives a lower percentage of clicks and incurs a hard cost to purchase keyword clicks, **you can be listed immediately** and are able to cover as **wide a range of terms** as your budget allows.

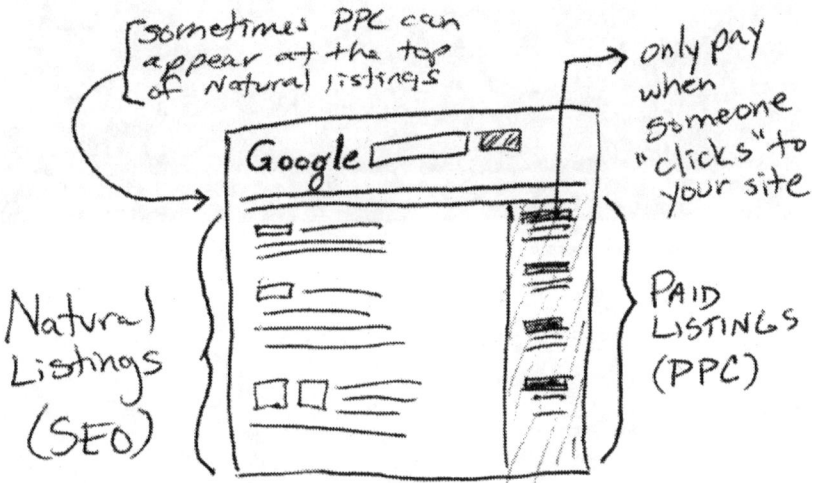

Search engine strategy is a very complex and deep practice in and of itself; so if you want to get serious about it, enlist a professional (see pages 64-66 for more info on hiring a professional firm). However, as an **absolute must have** for your business, do your best to ensure your site is at least **listed in natural search results for your business name**, otherwise your Web site investment was nearly worthless (see chart on next page).

Company Name Is The Most Commonly Used Keyword When Initially Launching a Search As a Result of Exposure to Some Offline Channel.

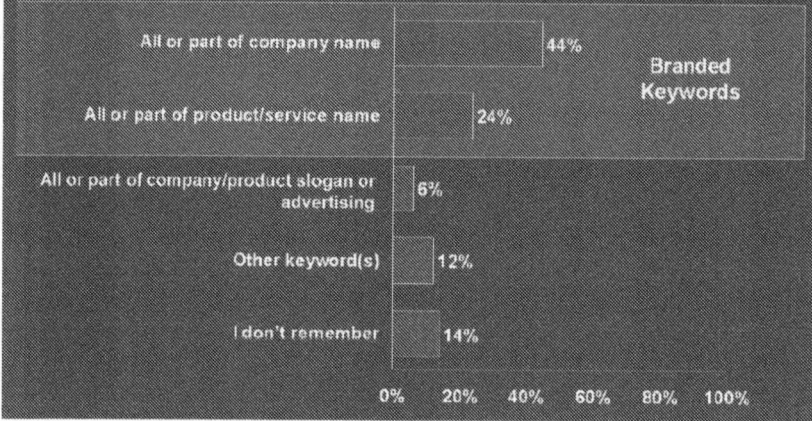

Keyword	Percentage
All or part of company name	44%
All or part of product/service name	24%
All or part of company/product slogan or advertising	6%
Other keyword(s)	12%
I don't remember	14%

Branded Keywords

iprospect.com & jupiterresearch.com

2. Media Buys

Also commonly referred to as banner ads, these appear most often on the right hand column, across the top and bottom of sites. Much like traditional billboards work on real roadways, **online banners serve to position your brand in front of desired demographics**. They focus more on brand penetration and awareness than on clicks to your site, but the more your customers see your brand, the higher the chance they will search for you and end up at your site one day. Check out how this multimedia approach works (online and offline) in the chart on the next page from a study conducted in August 2007.

Two-Thirds of Online Search Users Are Driven to Perform Searches As a Result of Exposure to Some Offline Channel. Both Television and Word of Mouth Influence Over One-Third.

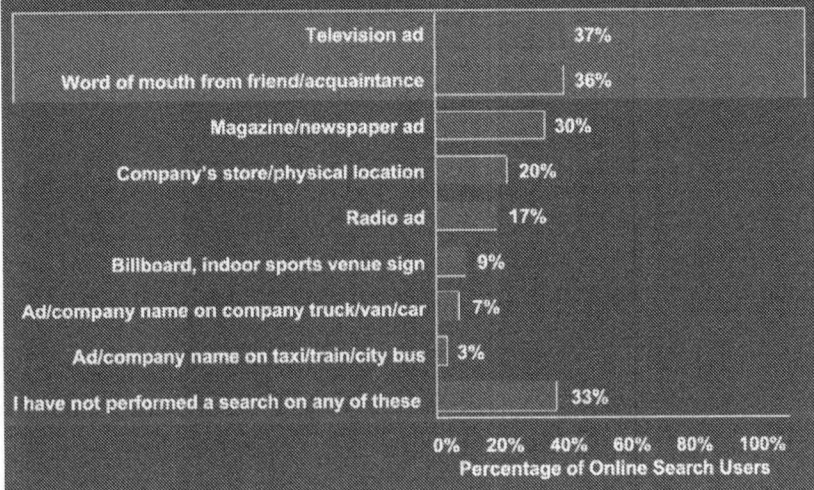

	Percentage of Online Search Users
Television ad	37%
Word of mouth from friend/acquaintance	36%
Magazine/newspaper ad	30%
Company's store/physical location	20%
Radio ad	17%
Billboard, indoor sports venue sign	9%
Ad/company name on company truck/van/car	7%
Ad/company name on taxi/train/city bus	3%
I have not performed a search on any of these	33%

iprospect.com & jupiterresearch.com

Many times, if you advertise offline in a newspaper or magazine, there is an online advertising counterpart that can enrich and broaden your coverage. Ask your advertising partners if they have such options and see what you can negotiate!

3. Social Media

The great world of social media not only helps with brand exposure, but is a huge contributor to natural search optimization in terms of providing additional search results and links back to your Web site. What is social media? The kids can tell you all about this one, since it's where they spend a good majority of their time these days (hopefully not on MySpace with the "To Catch a Predator" creeps).

Social media can be defined as a Web site that allows for user-centric communication such as sharing content, media, opinions and experiences. Some of the more popular social media sites include MySpace, Linked In, Digg, StumbleUpon, LiveJournal, Flickr, and You Tube. Think of it as your customers taking your brand, product and service into their own lives and creating what it means to them.

I know this sounds scary, but a successful social or viral (easily spread by people) media component to your offering, or around a specific campaign can provide amazing results. It did for Burger King in 2004 with the Subservient Chicken campaign (man in chicken costume does what you type in and tell him to do), generating countless visits, water cooler conversation, increasing traffic to the Burger King site and increasing sales of the targeted TenderCrisp Chicken Sandwich (**subservientchicken.com**).

Social media campaigns are great for building brand awareness, increasing customer loyalty, traffic to your site and building email lists. Just make sure you clearly identify your business objectives, research the target social media channel demographics to ensure they match your need, and determine the best way to engage people initially and ongoing, like I did at **youcantgetthere.com/iamhere**. The key is truly knowing your target.

Finding the Right Professional Firm

When do you need a firm to help? Anytime you are building anything larger than an online brochure for a mom and pop shop, especially when it comes to online marketing. The challenge in selecting the right firm is in knowing what questions to ask and what size and type of firm is right for you.

The next page provides a review of some of the leading industry online marketing agencies who can help you get there (seek their help if you are a Fortune 500 company or have a HUGE online presence).

If you don't need the big guns (and big price tags), I have created a few quick questions online for you to complete. Based on this info, I will be able to refer you to a qualified professional that best matches your needs, goals and budget.

My years of industry experience have allowed me to understand who is best at what, and which questions to ask. So let me do the heavy lifting for you, take out a lot of the guesswork and get you in contact with some awesome online experts! Think of it like eharmony.com for your online expert, as my vision is to pair up the best fits with one another. Visit **youcantgetthere.com/iamhere** to fill out the form today. It's a completely **FREE** service.

Select Paid Listing Agencies
Based on Business Value, Market Suitability and Agency Size

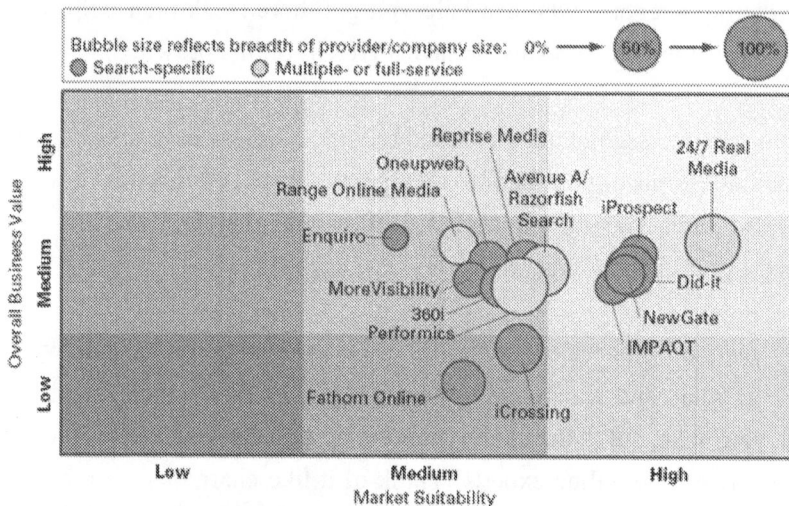

Bubble size reflects breadth of provider/company size: 0% ⟶ 50% ⟶ 100%
● Search-specific   ○ Multiple- or full-service

Overall Business Value — High / Medium / Low

Reprise Media
Oneupweb
Range Online Media
Avenue A/ Razorfish Search
24/7 Real Media
iProspect
Enquiro
MoreVisibility
360i
Performics
Did-it
NewGate
IMPAQT
Fathom Online
iCrossing

Low   Medium   High
Market Suitability

Select SEO Agencies
Based on Business Value, Market Suitability and Agency Size

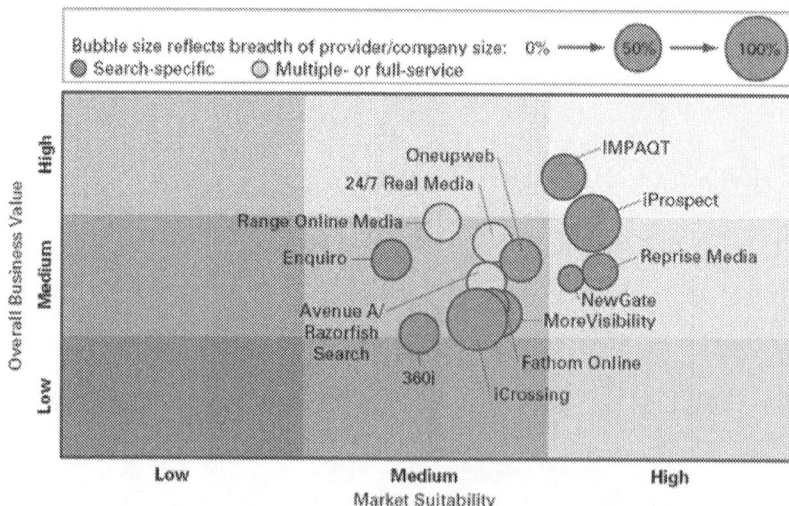

Bubble size reflects breadth of provider/company size: 0% ⟶ 50% ⟶ 100%
● Search-specific   ○ Multiple- or full-service

Overall Business Value — High / Medium / Low

IMPAQT
Oneupweb
24/7 Real Media
iProspect
Range Online Media
Enquiro
Reprise Media
Avenue A/ Razorfish Search
NewGate
MoreVisibility
360i
Fathom Online
iCrossing

Low   Medium   High
Market Suitability

Source: JupiterResearch (8/06) © 2006 JupiterResearch, a division of JupiterKagan, Inc.

▶ *Visit **youcantgetthere.com/iamhere** for "You Can't Get There from Here"*

You Can't Get There From Here: Complete Lyrics

We knew where we were goin',
Had it all mapped out
We followed the directions,
But the road was washed out

Tried to flip a quick bitch,
Only room for a three-point turn
That's when I thanked my lucky stars
My Dad taught driver's ed

Pulled off at the next gas station
To ask the best way around
That's when we first heard those unpleasant words
"You can't get there from here"

What kind of moron do you take me for?
As a crow flies, it's not that far
Your colloquialisms are cute and all
But I'm so sick of sitting' in this car

That's when I had an idea
And pulled out my iphone
I opened up a Google search
In the Web browser

I keyed in the place we were goin'
And hit search....and waited
No matches in the first five pages
I was about to give up

Oh look up there is a super Wal-Mart
I'm sure someone can help us
Really, how hard can it be?
Who wouldn't have heard about where were goin'?

"Please somebody help me
We're lookin' for the Chuck E. Cheese
The man at the gas station
And Google search both said the same thing"

You can't get there from here
You can't get there from here
You can't, you can't, you can't
Get there from here

6 To Make a Long Story Short…

Why is it that anytime someone begins with this, you just know you're in for it? You get the longest, most drawn-out, boring version of something that they could have said in 10 words or less.

In honor of this concept, this will be the shortest chapter of the book. There has been a plethora of research done on this topic (indexed in the references at the end of this book), but it all really boils down to:

1. People scan online, they don't read; **write to allow scanning** (avoid long, endless text blocks and be sure to take white space into consideration); ideally **hire a copywriter** skilled at writing for the Web
2. **Deliver on your promise**. "To make a long story short" really means, **make it SHORT**
3. Visually highlight keywords and **trigger words**
4. Use sub-headers to **chunk content**, and always make them **meaningful, not clever**
5. Opposite of writing a story, **get to the point first**, explain later
6. **Bullets** really can be the magic bullet online

Doodle and note-taking space

7 Best if Used by…

You labored for endless hours over copy. You tweaked this and that, then tweaked them both back again. You rewrote your company bios 10 times and finally received approval. You hope to never have to go through this again. You and your team have tested for 3 weeks straight and the day has finally arrived.

It's Go-Live Time!

Now what?

Six months pass, a year. You begin to notice things you'd like to change on the site. Two years pass, your competitors just redesigned their site and your boss is breathing down your neck. Why doesn't our site have this or that? Why didn't we do this or that when we launched our site?

You talk to your Internet team lead and relay the owner's concerns. Her recommendation from this conversation is to budget for a full redesign next year. "After all", she says, "Web sites are only designed to be **effective for 3-4 years at most**."

You can't believe what you are hearing and what you have to do. You can't imagine how your boss will react or that you have to deliver this news yourself. You bring this to your boss and leave thinking your job is on the line.

Here's the thing about Web sites and their relative life spans.

Many people think it's a one-time deal, or perhaps a once every 10 years type of thing. And the experts often forget to educate the client about a more realistic expectation early enough in the process. So here are a few comparisons to help with this exact challenge, since most Web sites should go through a significant redesign every 3-4 years, based on a number of factors outlined in this chapter.

Cell Phones and Laptops

I remember having a cell phone exactly like the one on the left circa 2001. I was hip and cool, just always frugal and settled for whatever phone came free with my Verizon plan. Now that I'm big time, I bought into the iPhone craze (still paying it off). You can see how far this market has come in 5-6 years, and from what I understand we in the U.S. are in the dark ages compared to Europe, Norway and some other super awesome places I have never had the privilege to visit.

I will pre-warn you that if you don't yet own an iPhone and don't feel like dropping a few hundo, DO NOT even play with one. That's what got me, and I'm so addicted now that I am certain I'll jump on the version 2.0 bandwagon as soon as it drives by!

Image courtesy of ecocycle.org   *Image courtesy of iPhone.com*

The combination of constant advances in technology, product marketing and our **insatiable desire to fill the holes in our hearts with more junk,** bring about new expectations for products and services in our world every day. And the way to continually serve our customers is to meet the demands of the market.

Images courtesy of Mac apple.com

The old Apple laptops appeared more like a toy than a business tool. It seems their clean design sensibilities have found a nice balance with the latest MacBook Pro on the right. Most professionals and home users replace their personal computers / laptops every 3 years as well, due to advances in technology, design, and the compatible mediums meant to run on such. Web sites have this life span for many of the same reasons.

Image courtesy of laptop.org

Interestingly enough, the $100 laptop program currently underway is bringing this child-like toy feeling back to life to service the world's children (above image). Their mission is to provide one laptop per child in the developing world where resources are severely lacking. Visit **laptop.org** yourself to learn more about this amazing project.

The purpose of the cell phone and laptop examples are to provide physical comparisons to a Web site to better illustrate the need to plan ahead for upgrades, enhancements and full redesigns.

After all, an outdated Web site is much like a Twinkie or used diapers buried in the landfill with no real chance for natural decomposition, just further polluting their surroundings and contaminating any good intention they may once have served.

Why 3 Years?

As a summary, the average 3-year Web site life span is due in part to:

1. Upgrades in Web browser standards
2. The standard life span of the personal computer
3. Advancing technology
4. Marketing trends
5. Consumerism
6. Planned obsolescence
7. The astrological alignment of Pluto and the Milky Way
8. Because I said so

So the next time you're working on a Web site, be sure you plan on and communicate this. And if you want to stay up to date on the latest trends, there are countless resources; here are some highlights:

- Browser, platform and display statistics: **w3schools.com/browsers**
- Online trends and statistics: **clickz.com/stats**
- Award-winning Web sites: **webbyawards.com**

And to make it easier on yourself, whenever possible, **subscribe to email updates or RSS feeds** on these sites so the content is delivered to your inbox or feed reader, instead of you having to remember to seek it out!

The beauty of the Internet…

Doodle and note-taking space

8 Junior High All Over Again

Every junior high and high school has cliques and drama. Here's where I sat in the overall scheme of things at mine:

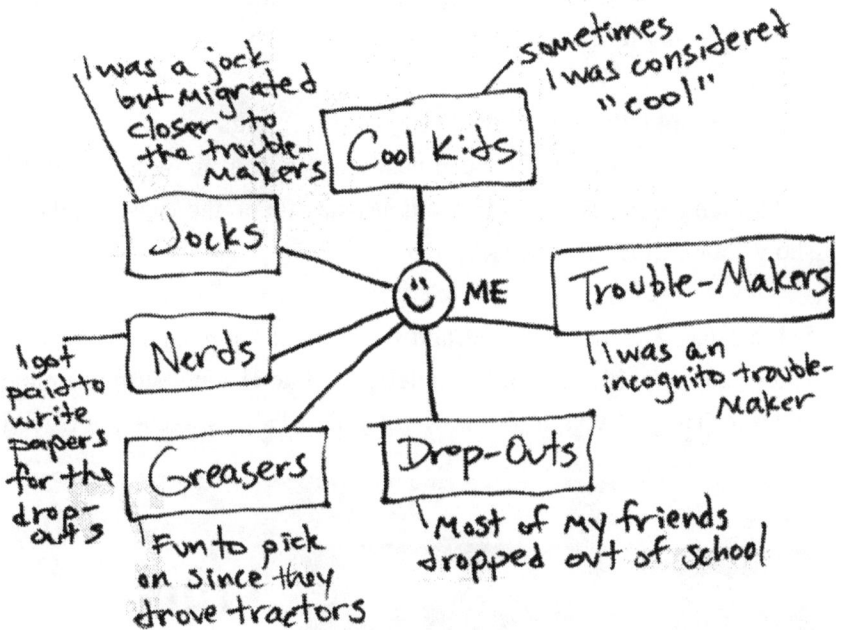

I was a jock but migrated closer to the trouble-makers

sometimes I was considered "cool"

Cool Kids

Jocks

ME

Trouble-Makers

Nerds

I was an incognito trouble-maker

I got paid to write papers for the drop-outs

Greasers

Drop-Outs

Fun to pick on since they drove tractors

Most of my friends dropped out of school

To be considered "cool" where I grew up, you had to be **popular** and **relevant**. I would guess that this is still true, but who knows, I could be way out of touch. I was always relevant, what with my nerd brain and direct connections to all other groups, but I wouldn't say I was ever the most popular. These two concepts are key to an online strategy.

Popularity

As much as I tried to be "too cool" to care if I was popular or not, I secretly wished I could have been Homecoming Queen. What's nice about the Internet is you can be the most popular without being the prettiest or sleeping around. More often than not, the nerdiest are the ones that get to be the most popular online. At last, I found my niche where **it's cool to be nerdy!**

Online popularity can be fleeting, just like in high school if you don't keep yourself relevant. You can easily see a drop in Web site traffic and search engine rankings if you don't stay up on the latest trends and show your online user base some love.

Some great sites to get listed and be deemed "popular" on are Digg (sites people online "dig"), StumbleUpon (like channel surfing online) and You Tube (if you don't know what You Tube is, come out of your box).

You need to **follow the standards and trends**, just like back in the day when you knew you looked awful with feathered bangs and pegged jeans, but did it anyway. Otherwise no one would even listen to you. The same is true online. Follow the leading trends, but just like back in high school, if you can be on the cutting edge of a trend or actually start one, that's when the big payoffs happen.

Relevancy

Do you know the latest gossip in your industry? Where do your customers read about you? What rumors have they heard? What are they saying about you? Do you need to send them a note to meet you after school in the parking lot to tell it to your face?

Where have you placed yourself in the market? Are you an expert in your field, or a follower and how does this effect how you are perceived? Do you even show up at the cool parties anymore?

Search engines are the ultimate judges of relevancy online. They are like your friendly librarians of days past when you were too lazy to use the Dewey Decimal System. "Where can I find such and such?" Google knows!

Your Web site needs to be listed on the major search engines for all the gossip and words that your customers are using.

First, find out what names they call you, how they find you, what they are looking for. Maybe even allow them to provide anonymous feedback surrounding such (add a Web site feedback form or perform an anonymous customer survey) so there is no threat of a sucker punch to the gut.

Another great place to find out what key terms your customers use to get to your site is within your Web analytics. Most analytics packages have a **"Search Term Referral" report** that shows you exactly which key terms were used to send how many visitors to your site. Wrap your arms around this and use it to refine your search engine strategy!

After you have all this information, ensure your Web site content, meta data, and external sites linking to you speak to this.

Then you'll certainly be the coolest kid in town!

9 In the Eyes of a Search Engine

▶ *Visit **youcantgetthere.com/iamhere** for "In the Eyes of a Search Engine"*

The concept for this chapter actually began with the song inspiration. I was discussing a client's search engine strategy with a colleague when he began, "so in the eyes of a search engine…" I immediately stopped him and had to make a mental note to recall this phrase as I could already hear the sappy country-style lyrics in my head.

So the true inspiration went something like this:

There really is a new realm of understanding once you see how a search engine views your Web site. It will make more sense why we tell you to stop cramming so many images on the pages or adamantly protest use of tables in code and "skip intro" animations on your site.

Let's use some real Web sites as samples for this chapter.

As a start, you need to write compliant code (as discussed earlier) in the accepted grammar of the Web (**validator.w3.org**), so you are 'speaking the same language' as search engines.

Once you are speaking the same language, you need to ensure that this language makes more sense than a mumbling drunk giving you directions home.

Take a look at what we as people see when we visit **levis.com**

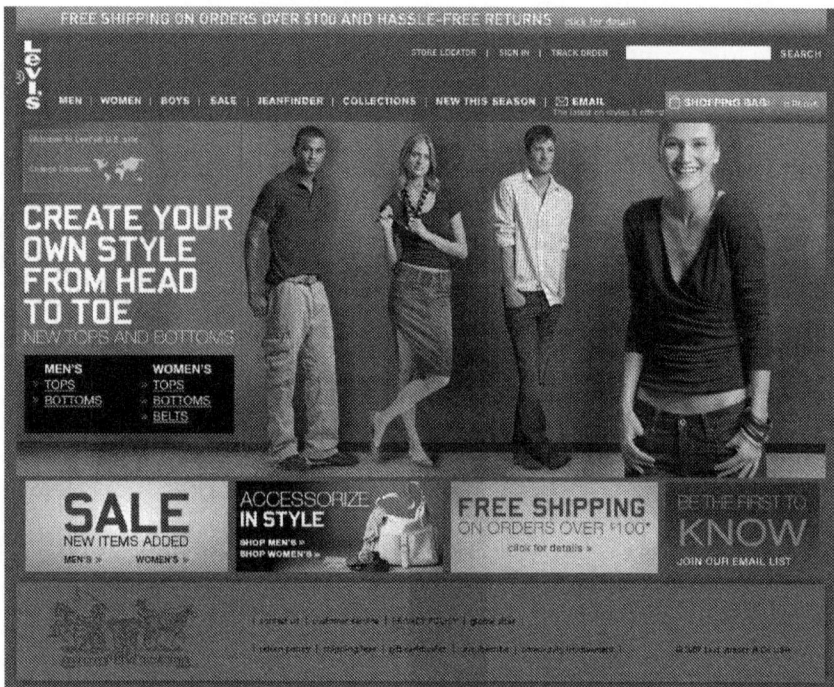

Pretty nice design, nice promotions for me to click deeper into the site. I can browse by the large image promotions or enter by category at the top. I know where I am with the recognizable Levis logo at the top. Not the best, but overall good when looking at it with my human eyes.

And here is how a search engine views it.

Levis.com

SEARCH

- SIZE FINDER
- SIGN IN
- SEARCH
- MEN
- WOMEN
- BOYS
- SALE
- JEANFINDER
- COLLECTIONS
- NEW THIS SEASON
- EMAIL

0 Items

CREATE YOUR OWN STYLE FROM HEAD TO TOE
NEW TOPS AND BOTTOMS

MEN'S   WOMEN'S
TOPS   TOPS
BOTTOMS   BOTTOMS
             BELTS

SALE
NEW ITEMS ADDED
MEN'S »   WOMEN'S »

ACCESSORIZE IN STYLE
SHOP MEN'S »
SHOP WOMEN'S »

FREE SHIPPING
ON ORDERS OVER $100*
click for details »

BE THE FIRST TO KNOW
JOIN OUR EMAIL LIST

contact us
customer service
PRIVACY POLICY
global sites
return policy
shipping fees
gift certificates
unsubscribe
community involvement
© 2007 Levi Strauss & Co USA

Not bad at first you say? But wait! **Search engines can't garner any meaning from images** without the hidden from the human eye descriptive text (called Alternate text) entered behind the scenes. The main design images, as well as all of the category navigation across the top are created using images, most of which have no descriptive text entered at all. In essence, all the search engine can read from this page is the following:

> Levis.com
> 0 Items
> contact us
> customer service
> PRIVACY POLICY
> global sites
> return policy
> shipping fees
> gift certificates
> unsubscribe
> community involvement
> © 2007 Levi Strauss & Co USA

For a search engine, looking to find relevant key terms and phrases, this doesn't bode well for Levis. Of course, with a name brand like Levis, practices like this are not as important as they are to the majority of small businesses out there with a greater need to drive search engine traffic.

Now lets take a look at how this looks when done correctly, or at least not quite as poorly.

Take a look at what we as people see when we visit **ikea.com**

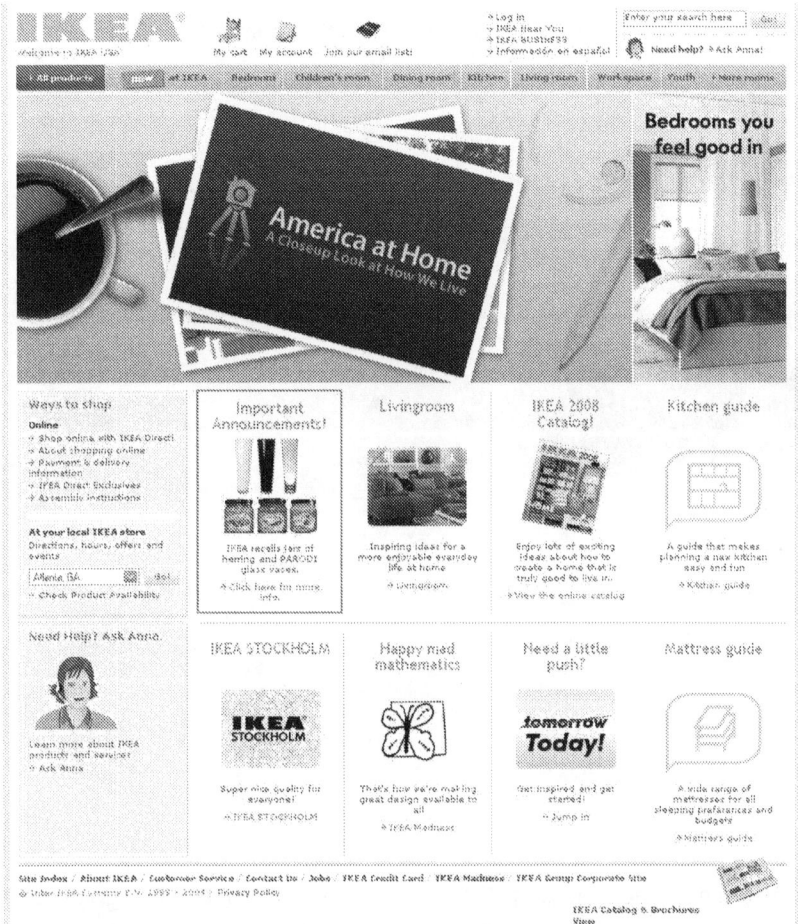

I see a very nice, clean layout. I have a lot of options to engage with the site including specials, online help, or if I know exactly what I want, I can enter via that room category or enter my keywords into the search in the upper right.

And here is how a search engine views the IKEA site. I split it into two columns so it is viewable on one page, though it still comes out looking incredibly small due to the amount of readable content on the page.

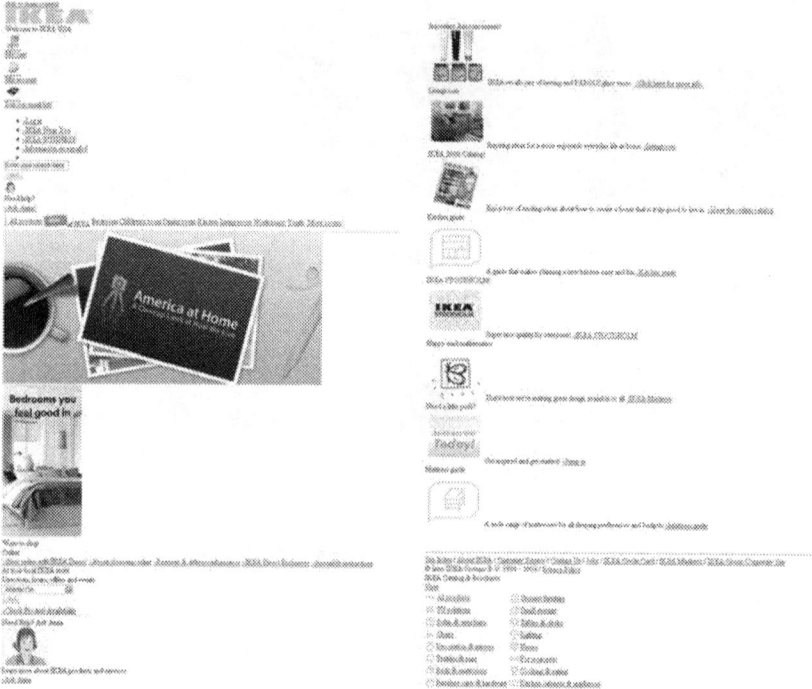

"Wow, that's more like it!" exclaims Google. There is a great deal more relevant and rich text content for search engines to eat up in this site. I am by no means pointing to the IKEA site as the perfect example, but the coding methodologies used here are far superior to those employed on the Levis site. It appears that IKEA is more concerned with being indexed on search engines, so great job!

They do a hit and miss job of consistently entering the hidden descriptive text for images, but just look at how many keywords they have packed into just the very bottom of this page.

Bathroom
Basement, garage, attic
Hallway & entrance
Laundry room

→ All products
▦ TV solutions
▭ Sofas & armchairs
h Chairs
△ Decoration & mirrors
▱ Textiles & rugs
▱ Beds & mattresses
◎ Furniture care & hardware
▱ Bathroom furniture
♘ Children's IKEA

▤ Storage furniture
▱ Small storage
♀ Tables & desks
♀ Lighting
▥ Floors
∞ For your pets
♀ Cooking & eating
▱ Kitchen cabinets & appliances
▯ Clothes storage
▥ Safety products

You can begin to get a sense for how much more relevant a properly coded site is to a search engine. And if its relevant to Google or Yahoo, larger numbers of qualified customers searching for these specific terms will find what they are looking for, ultimately driving business your way.

▶ *Visit **youcantgetthere.com/iamhere** for "In the Eyes of a Search Engine"*

In the Eyes of a Search Engine: Complete Lyrics
I logged online about 10pm
Wonderin' when my mud flaps would deliver
They already charged my credit card
and Lord knows I been workin' hard
All winter

I'd like to get me one of those
Matchin', NASCAR air freshners
So I typed me up into Google
"Discount NASCAR Air Freshners"

Soon as I hit that search button
I was overwhelmed with nothin'
I'd heard of

I didn't see me no Chevy
Marlboro, or KFC
In the listings

That's when I called my old lady
To come in and work her
Google magic
She works on computers all day
And knows how to have her way
Online

And here's what she told me:

"Honey, you just gotta' understand
Search engines ain't just some kinda' man

They're kinda' like your pick-up truck
Battered, bruised and broken-up
Stutterin' and hickin'-up
Looking for some words of love
Love

Through the eyes of a search engine
Your words, they mean everything
No pretty words or pick-up lines
Are gonna' help you to find
The search result to change your life
Like the site that made us man and wife
If you're relevant and poplar
The search engines will praise your worth
Rewarding you with page one listings

Page one, page one
Everybody wants page one
Page one, page one
Get me to the top of page one

If I'm not on page one, what am I paying you for?
Page one…"

Doodle and note-taking space

10 We're Thinking of Adding an Addition

Yes, I know the title of this chapter is repetitive. "Adding an addition", but that is literally what people say. I wonder if a double positive makes a negative, like when you say, "I don't NOT want to go", which really means you want to, or you are a passive aggressive pussy.

Anyway, I consider this one **the barnburner of all analogies** ever conceived and shared about Web sites. You guessed it, **the house** analogy. But darn, it's a good one.

I first began this discussion of a Web site as a building with colleagues in Pittsburgh, PA back in 1998. We were hunting for a 'simple to explain' and 'simpler to understand' elevator pitch about what the Internet was.

Ever since I was a little girl, my father dropped hints that I should become an architect (spending countless school vacations driving to see first-hand the architectural wonders of Frank Lloyd Wright from Falling Water to Taliesin), so maybe this is my mind's subliminal means of bringing that forth.

This conversation continued to my days in Phoenix, AZ and even made its way into the branded template names that I assigned to my 11"x17" information architecture schemas. These behemoth and hair-splitting labors of love and hate took on a life of their own, almost driving me to the brink of insanity. To this day, seeing that many boxes, arrows, labels and symbols give me the shakes.

I referred to these marvels as the site **blueprint**, the high-level diagrams as the site outline (like an **elevation**) and the detailed page-level view as wire frames (like a **floor plan**).

I can even recall discussions about how user flow diagrams are much like environmental design and architectural space flow and usage charts.

Almost any way you slice it, the house / building analogy works wonders for explaining the logic of Web site design to people. Here is a brief glimpse of one of my infamous site **blueprint** documents:

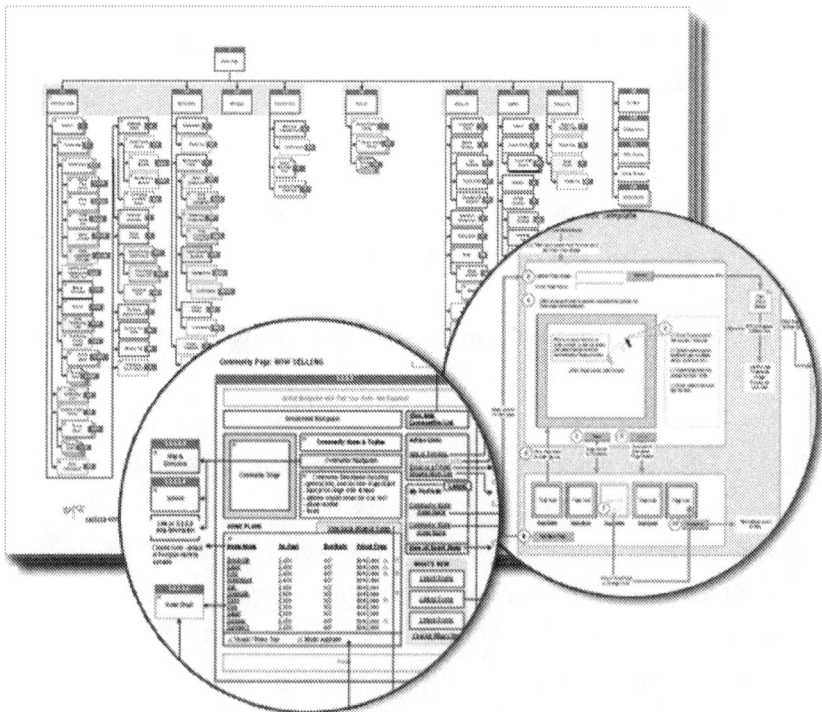

This super detailed practice of documentation has been scaled back a bit in recent days within the industry, with more focus on getting to the actual interactive tool to use as a working model and prototype. A wonderful resource for this approach was published as a book by 37signals called "Getting Real", available for purchase online at **gettingreal.37signals.com**.

At my most recent company as a Managing Director, I heard the house as Web site analogy elegantly referenced time and again by our CEO as a successful sales tool. I knew I had landed at the right firm when I heard her speak these magical words, a bit **like coming home again...**

And here is a glossary of how you can use this analogy to better understand and/or sell the thought process of designing a Web site.

The Value of Planning and Project Management

You would never conceive of building a home without detailed plans for everything from the plumbing and electrical to the landscape. And what sort of lunatic would start with selecting the interior paint colors?

Sadly enough, this is where many people think Web sites do begin, as a visual design concept, when this is actually one of the last things to occur. In my experience, **the planning phases of an Internet project are one of the most important, but most highly protested and least understood**. The plan for the project is the foundation of tested stability and principles of **structural integrity** upon which the entire Web site strategy rests.

Once a strong foundation is in place, all of the functional and aesthetic layers can be applied.

Project Management is your General Contractor, working with all the specialists to ensure the project is completed on time and on budget. Otherwise, you could end up with a breathtaking new home and nowhere to make a deposit. Someone needs to plan for the bathrooms!

Planning for a Big Family

A great architect knows how to construct a home to exist perfectly on its own and be fully functional for a young married couple, but easily allow for any future additions. A 2 bedroom, 1 bath starter home, planned correctly, can become a 4 bedroom, 2 bath family residence.

However, if this intention is not uncovered or discussed before the first version is constructed, you may discover some unpleasant news once little Bubba is on the way. Your contractor may inform you that the exterior wall on the side of the house with the most lot space available for expansion has no plumbing readily available. Anyone who has even dabbled in home remodeling is familiar with the type of nightmares hiding behind walls and beneath carpets.

The same is true for a Web site. If an extendible technical and information architecture is not conceived of prior to the initial build, you can find yourself hammering on additions and repurposing sections until you're left with an eyesore on the neighborhood (yeah, that's where the crazy people live, don't go near it).

Custom trailer with roof deck

Ocean-front home

Two nice examples of poor planning (or lack of adequate zoning) can be found in the snapshots above, taken on a trip to Mexico. The left is a trailer with a winding staircase and rooftop sun deck. The one on the right is at least one trailer covered in stucco to "blend-in". Oh, and it's for sale! I will be nice and not call out any Web site examples of these atrocities but hopefully you get the picture.

Windows and Doors

Perfect analogy for **entry and exit points** for your Web site.

Emergency Exit Plans and Signage

High-rise buildings have detailed emergency exit plans. Your Web site needs something similar, what we refer to as **way-finding systems**. A fun exercise, or test I like to use with this one is to imagine you are kidnapped, blindfolded and dropped in the middle of a building you have never been in before. What do you do to figure out where you are, where to go, the way out?

This is a pretty common scenario online. **We don't always land on a Web site's home page**. Often times we enter via a side door or porch window and then have no idea where to go from there. A few simple tools to employ on your site to help users with this are:

1. Logo and Tagline: what building am I in and what do you do?
2. Select State and Page Title: where am I exactly in the building?
3. Breadcrumb Navigation: what is the way back out?

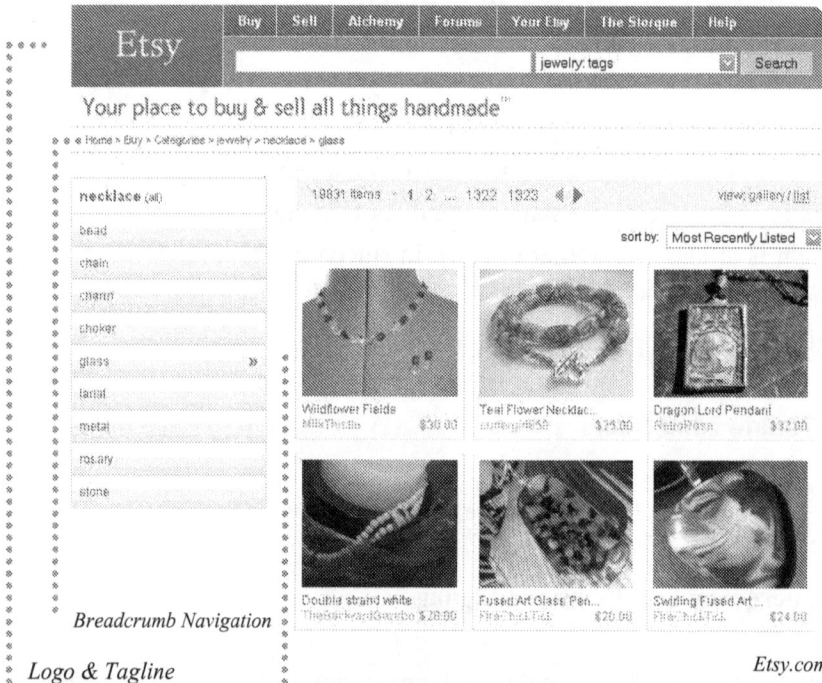

Breadcrumb Navigation

Logo & Tagline   Etsy.com

Select State for "glass"

This "emergency exit" practice is often referred to as **"contingency design"** in the Internet industry. 37signals has also published a **FREE** and practical white paper on this practice including how to help people when things go wrong. Get it at **37signals.com/whitepaper**.

I took one liberty with the 'Etsy' screen shot above. I added in the tagline from the home page "Your place to buy and sell all things handmade" to this interior page. This would help greatly for visitors entering via an internal page to get a sense of what the site has to offer. Another addition that would help is a page title, since now they are relying on the left-hand navigation select state for "glass" as such. Overall though, great job!

Another awesome feature on this site and great use of animation online is the browse by color section. As you move your mouse around the screen, the color swatches get larger and the search results allow you to browse products by color, really cool, see for yourself: **etsy.com/color**

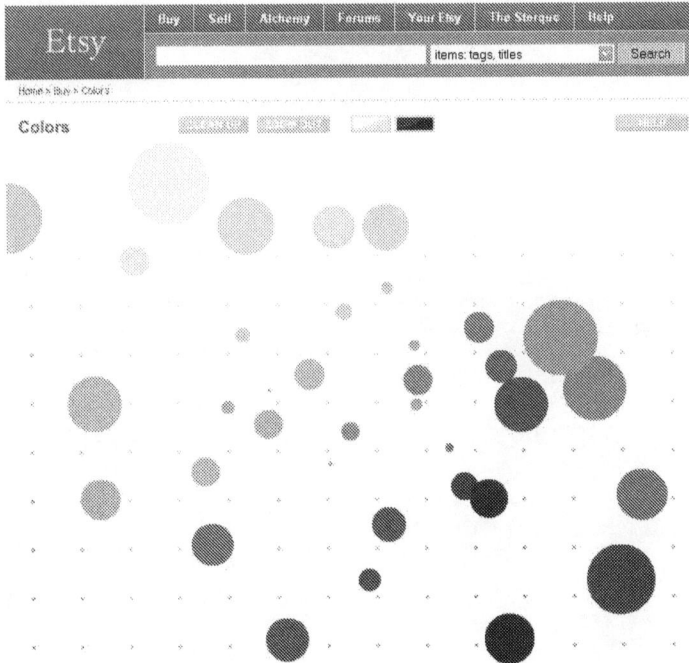

Etsy.com

Play around with it; come up with your own house / Internet comparisons. Use it three times and it's yours!

Doodle and note-taking space

11 Meatloaf Again?!?

Maybe you are a fan of meatloaf (the sorry excuse for something edible, or the sorry excuse for something audible in the larger-than-life rock-opera singer). Me, not so much.

This topic is an oldie, but a goodie: **Mystery Meat Navigation**.

I can thankfully say that I don't come across this phenomenon as often as I used to, but it still finds its way onto some pretty big name Web sites.

What is it you ask?

Much like ordering 'chicken' in the nether regions of Mexico or negotiating your younger college-age brother's 'leftover casserole special', you're **never quite sure what you've gotten yourself into**.

Mystery Meat Navigation typically requires you to mouse-over an image to then learn what you will get by clicking. I don't know whose ingenious idea this is of fun, but it's outright moronic in a world where we lose interest faster than panties fly at a Tom Jones concert.

Another example of this is labeling something with a vague title (like "Stuff", "Miscellaneous", "Information", or "History and Mystery for $600") so that when you click into the section, you want out of there faster than last night's spicy Mexican food. ('Faster than' similes are fun!)

Some examples of mystery meat navigation:

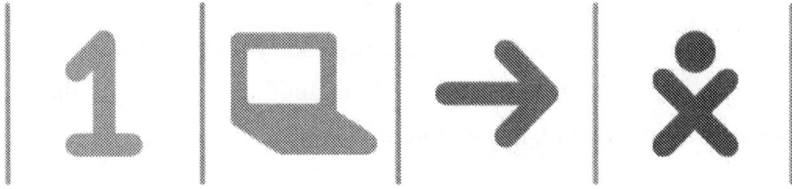

Laptop.org Home Page: that is seriously all that appears on the page

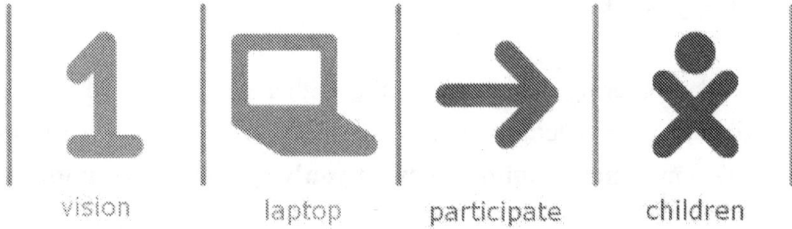

vision   laptop   participate   children

Laptop.org Home Page: After rolling over each item individually, hmmm…

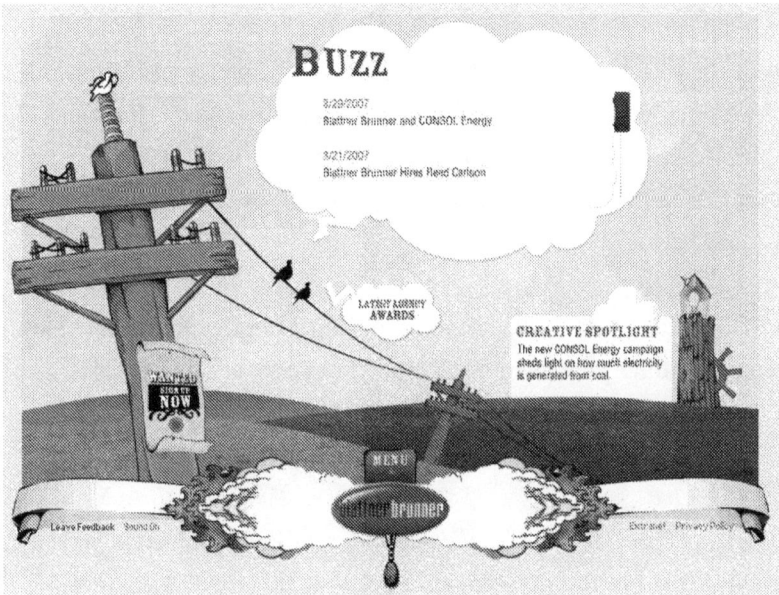

Wow, can you find the navigation? I actually used to work for a division of this company too: blattnerbrunner.com

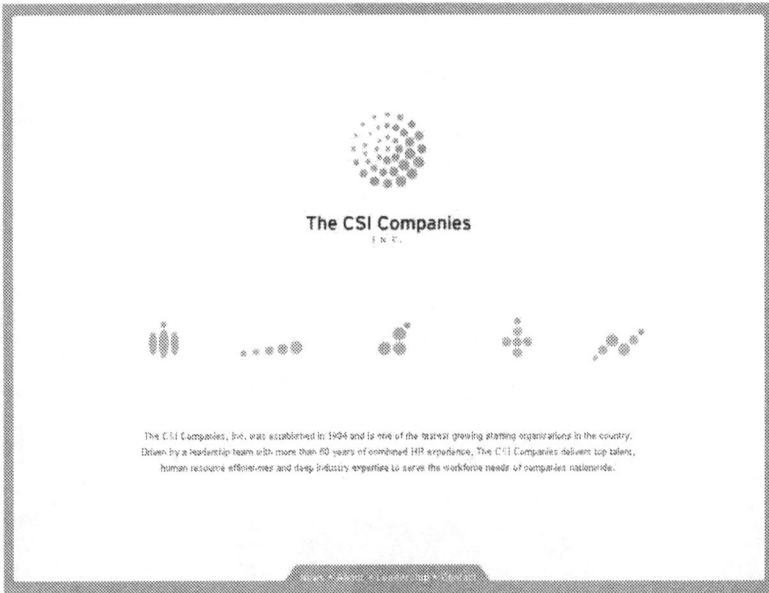

Is it online Braille? customstaffinginc.com

I can't take credit for finding this last one (CSI Companies). It is indexed on **webpagesthatsuck.com**, which is a pretty useful site that even provides checklists to find out for yourself if your site sucks. In fact, the site's owner, Vincent Flanders, claims to have coined the term 'Mystery Meat Navigation' and wikipedia gives him credit as well. Way to go Vincent!

I hate to break it to him, because his site does offer some useful content, including published books, but I have to say that the site itself sucks pretty hard (whoops, did I say that?). I can only hope that he is trying to demonstrate by example how to design poorly.

Come on people, it's 2007, we should really know better by now. **Please don't serve the mystery meat** or hide the goodies anymore.

12 Google is the New Kleenex

If you haven't heard, or personally used the expression "Google it," then you must be Amish (I grew up near a ton of Mennonites, a milder form of Amish, "Amish Light" if you will, from what I understand, in Upstate NY; their pies, bread and quilts are unrivaled).

In the U.S., **Google outranks Yahoo**, the runner-up in terms of search volume, **by almost 3x**! This would be like running a mile in 5 minutes and the second place runner finished in just under 15 minutes. No wonder Google has become a household name.

Rank	Search Engine	Volume
1.	www.google.com	64.14%
2.	search.yahoo.com	22.88%
3.	search.msn.com	6.59%
4.	www.ask.com	3.35%

Source - Hitwise - August, 2007 - based on volume of searches.

hitwise.com/datacenter/searchengineanalysis.php

Consumer markets throughout time have shown that when a brand name becomes strong enough and dominates the majority of the market, it is possible to "verb-alize" the brand into a new lexicon within our language. Some great examples of this are

Kleenex	>	Tissue
Coke	>	Soda / Pop
Xerox	>	Photocopy
Google	>	Online Search

There are tons more, see if you can name ten!

A study was conducted in 2002-2003 by an Oklahoma University, to learn what people in various regions of the U.S. call the fizzy carbonated sweet drink we Americans chug down by the Big Gulp.

I was first introduced to this study in training given by Indi Young and Peter Merholz of Adaptive Path. To this day, I still use it as a shining example of how people do not in fact speak the same language and how important labeling is online. The map below shows the usage of "Pop" (blue), "Coke" (appropriately Red) and "Soda" (Yellow), the top 3 most popular names for this carbonated beverage across the U.S.

View the full color version at popvssoda.com or on the book companion site at **youcantgetthere.com/iamhere.**

This explains why I always feel so torn as to whether I call it "Pop" or "Soda" since I was born and raised right on the Pop/Soda blue/yellow border in upstate NY. It also confirms that the south is, in general, a bit of an embarrassment. I have asked many people from the southern states, since seeing this chart, how they would order a soft drink. Amazingly, many of them respond something like, "I'll have a Coke, a Sprite."

Wow, just wow…Coke must have pumped a lot of money into The South. I don't really understand it, but again, I'm not from there, so to each his or her own I guess.

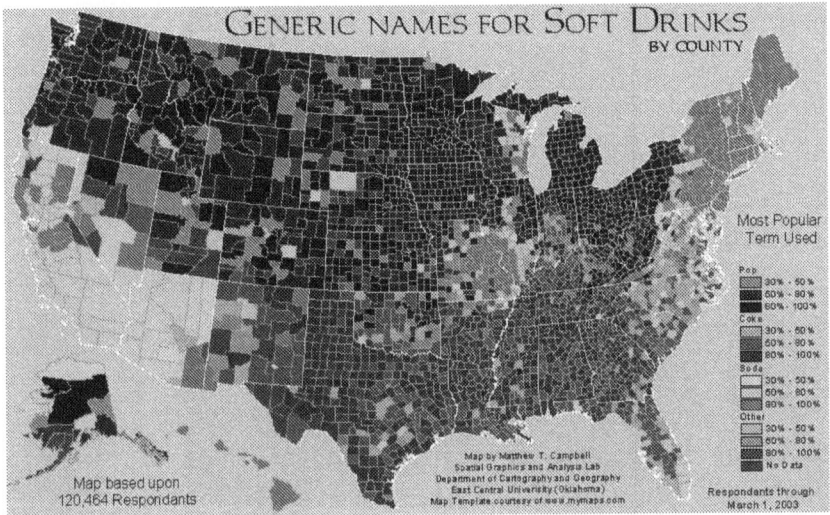

GENERIC NAMES FOR SOFT DRINKS
BY COUNTY

Most Popular
Term Used

Pop
30% - 50%
50% - 80%
80% - 100%

Coke
30% - 50%
50% - 80%
80% - 100%

Soda
30% - 50%
50% - 80%
80% - 100%

Other
30% - 50%
50% - 80%
80% - 100%
No Data

Map by Matthew T. Campbell
Spatial Graphics and Analysis Lab
Department of Cartography and Geography
East Central University (Oklahoma)
Map Template courtesy of www.mymaps.com

Map based upon
120,464 Respondants

Respondants through
March 1, 2003

popvssoda.com

Another amusing anecdote I can share about The South is a conversation I had with a Mexican beach vendor while on vacation down there. I recently purchased property in Rocky Point, and so am trying to become more fluent at speaking the language and learning the culture. For this reason, I constantly strike up conversations with the locals. Plus, they absolutely love us Americans. It's a nice break from the attitude problems, sense of entitlement, and overall lack of respect in this country (God Bless America, I do love the freedoms afforded here, please don't come after me).

Anyway, I was talking to this guy, and asked him if he has ever been to the U.S. He said, "Jes, I swim across Rio Grande and go to Alabama". I absolutely love how Mexicans say "yes"; anything with the Y/J combination is fun. I was in a mobile phone store in Phoenix one day asking about web browsing capabilities with a phone and the merchant kept saying that "jes, eet works weeth jahoo". I was so confused, and then I finally got it and felt like a complete ass. We chuckled; it was cute.

So anyway, as soon as the beach vendor said he had ended up in The South, I stopped him saying, "Oh man, that isn't the U.S. That's like another country."

He continued, "jes, I get that feeling because I work construction and only who work are me and the black guy while others just sit around." We chuckled; it was cute. I asked him to please not judge all Americans by that standard to which he replied that he understood the difference in The South and said that if he ever goes back to the U.S. he will visit another area instead.

The point of this chapter, though a bit wandering, is that **Google is big poppa** and leading many fields, not just online search. So if you ever need to know where markets are going, **keep an eye on Google**.

Also, I am hopeful that someday Carissa and Viv (my nickname) will be synonymous with Renaissance Prophet.

13 Pig Latin

I was never fortunate enough as a child to become fluent in pig Latin, though I know I have made up my fair share of words over the years, most too dirty to share here.

what is said → What is heard

This final chapter is dedicated to the bizarre, often comical language of the Internet, all of its acronyms, invented terms and completely unrealistic expectations. You can also find a similar and fun tool online at **dack.com/web/bullshit.html**

The following is a rough translation of various Internet-isms:

Internet-ism	True Meaning
Simply log on to our Web site at…	I am very ignorant in all things Internet, what I meant to say is "Visit our site at…" since you are rarely required to login to a home page
It sounds like a server-side error	I have no idea what is wrong and am not technical at all, in fact I also believe your car's got a cracked block
I want the design to "POP"	I have no experience in design technique or theory, but have a degree in Marketing from a trade school
We seamlessly integrate with your company, becoming a natural extension of your Marketing team	Just sign the contract so I can get my commission
Our site gets over 50 Million hits every single month	Hits (file queries) are a nearly meaningless web metric and with a number that high, unless you are eBay, your site most likely has something very wrong with it
We build everything in LINUX within a Gnome environment using Kernal Patches and the Motif GUI	Because I am an IT professional I must constantly demonstrate how inferior you are to me

Internet-ism	True Meaning
Our site needs a blog, AJAX, an interactive site host that talks to the visitor, and music, lots of music	I am so addicted to buzz that I have sprouted wings and make honey; I am completely out of touch with what my customers want or need and honestly don't care, so just throw as much heaping, steaming crap up there as you can
Our site needs to be crisp, clean, usable and easy to navigate	When I purchase this car, make sure it has tires and a steering wheel
Our site requirements are fairly simple: real-time synching with our legacy back-end inventory database, automated intelligent email marketing campaigns tied to offline triggers at the point of purchase, merging 8 separate product sets and SKUs into one seamless online listing with full interactive customizable options for the online shoppers; and our delivery timeline is 10 weeks from now as we will unveil this at the annual shareholders conference	My head is up my arse

Thanks for playing!

And don't forget to visit **youcantgetthere.com/iamhere** to contribute to the blog, watch the videos or get **FREE** help finding the best firm to help you achieve online success.

Ten-four, over and out....

Open Book Quiz

This quiz is meant to be fun, so don't sigh all depressed-like. Plus, the book is right here in front of you, you slacker. This can help you recall the topics we covered as well as provide you an opportunity to prove exactly how smart you are smarty-pants (or if you want to cheat, get answers at **youcantgetthere.com/iamhere**)!

1. What do the following acronyms represent in the online world?
   - IA _____
   - SEO _____
   - PPC _____
   - SEM _____
   - AOV _____
   - CPL _____

2. Create 3 of your own 'Faster than' similes. I'll get you started:
   - Faster than panties fly at a Tom Jones concert
   - Faster than _____
   - Faster than _____
   - Faster than _____

3. What is the average **offline** shopping conversion rate compared to the average **online** rate range?

4. **Draw** your own kitchen, backyard, home floor plan or neighborhood. Then create a site map of your sketch as it would exist online. Keep in mind the various levels of information and how each of the users interacts differently with such. There are no wrong answers here, just give it a try! Do this exercise at work with your teammates!

5. Visit your company's Web site and some of your competitors. See if you can identify the primary, secondary and tertiary navigation systems. Print out the page and label 1, 2 and 3 in terms of visual importance. Have family members or others not familiar with what you do try it as well. **Do they match your business goals?**

6. Do you notice examples of **chunking** or **hierarchy**? Are there any obvious violations to these rules or areas of improvement you can identify?

7. Do you know your key site metrics? If not, see if you can gather the following:
    ◦   Total Monthly Visits   _____
    ◦   Total Conversions   _____
    ◦   Conversion Rate   _____
    ◦   Cost Per Lead / Sale   _____
    ◦   Cost Per Lead by Referral Source_____

8. Is your site written in valid and compliant code? Enter the URL into **validator.w3.org** and find out!

9. **Can the search engines find your site?** Do some samples searches in Google and Yahoo with your company's name, key products, services and geographical areas served. Do you come up in the first page of listings? Does your search engine listing adequately inform the visitor so he/she can make an intelligent decision to click through to your site or not?

10. Does the writing on your Web site **bore the crap** out of you? Does it need an overhaul to better comply with how we read online?

11. When was your company's Web site last redesigned? If it was more than 3 years, you may be in need of an overhaul. Visit youcantgetthere.com/iamhere and complete the simple questions so I can find a great partner for you. And it's totally **FREE**!

12. Are you **popular** and **relevant**? Who is talking about you where? Try this neat trick to see who is linking to you: Go to google.com and type "**link:**http://www.yoursite.com" into the search box. The resulting listings will show a comprehensive list of all the Web sites linking to you as indexed by Google.

13. Navigate to a secondary or tertiary level page deep within your site and see if you can **identify the following** way finding elements:
    ◦ Logo and Tagline   _____
    ◦ Select State and Page Title_____
    ◦ Breadcrumb Navigation _____

14. Is there any **mystery meat navigation** lurking on your site? Can you find other sites that still rely on this ostracized practice?

15. We reviewed the Google/Kleenex analogy. I mentioned wanting to eventually become identified with "Renaissance Prophet". **What is your brand strength**? What terms, products, services or phrases do you strive to stand for? Can you launch an online marketing campaign to build and support this, perhaps using social marketing networks?

16. **Bonus challenge** for extra credit

Do you need more love from your Internet firm? Do you need to give them more love? Go **hug an Internet professional today**; heck, hug 2 or 3!

Hopefully these exercises give you enough ammo to make some improvements to your site, or even push through a full redesign effort of online marketing strategy. **Be sure to take your research and edits needed to the decision makers!**

Remember to check your answers at **youcantgetthere.com/iamhere**. Good luck!

About Me: Unabridged

This is my first book, so forgive me for going on a bit much. From a young age, I always knew I was different; good different. I knew it was my destiny to make a meaningful impact in the world. I am still creating what that is each and every day, but this book is one expression of that drive.

I grew up in rural upstate New York, in the Finger Lakes Region, attended college at Carnegie Mellon University in Pittsburgh, PA. NY and PA can be very beautiful 3 months out of the year, but since I hate the cold and lack of sunshine, I now split my time between Arizona and Mexico. My folks raised me as the typical rural upstate NY kid: naked, grounded and listening to sixties folk and rock music: Neil Young, Grateful Dead, Beatles and Jethro Tull are still among my favorites. The place I grew up, the people I knew and the music I absorbed helped shape me into the person I am today, and continue to influence my art and life.

What else is there to tell? Well, I like long walks on the beach, relaxing dinners and some good Barry White (kidding sicko, plus I'm taken!)

As you have seen if you viewed the accompanying online educational music videos, I play acoustic rhythm guitar and consider myself a better songwriter and singer than guitarist. My music is a source of strength, healing, celebration and laughter. I love photography, particularly of people, seeing their essence and spirit through the lens. I am an active individual, spending my time practicing Bikram Yoga, hiking and bicycling. Basically, I have trouble sitting still and am constantly immersed in one project or another. Mostly, I enjoy hanging out on my own, listening to tunes, creating things and thinking of my next big idea.

I spend a lot of time with my dogs (a.k.a. "my girls"). They are great companions. I like to just sit and observe them, cuddle with them and make up languages based on their barks (bork, rarf, snarf, etc.). You'd be surprised how much you can learn from a dog (give me a break; I have no kids yet.) If you want to know more than that, I guess you'll just have to move to Arizona and start hanging out with me (no stalkers welcome, my boyfriend owns a Smith & Wesson .357 magnum, though I hate guns).

My proudest achievements include
- Winning a county drawing contest in elementary school
- Graduating second in my high school class while being a punk-ass
- Graduating with honors from Carnegie Melon University
- Kicking through a 2x4 in Tae Kwon Do
- Completing a 100-Mile charity bike ride on a torn knee
- Hiking the Grand Canyon Rim-to-Rim alone in one day
- The look of appreciation and love on people's faces every time I give them a homemade gift or photo of their children
- Having the courage to follow my dreams and just jump

Still to be accomplished

◦ Bicycle across the United States

◦ Give my parents back more than they have given me

◦ Hike the Appalachian Trail with my brother

◦ Visit a country other than the US, Canada or Mexico

◦ Drive the entire Mexican coast and boat the Sea of Cortez

◦ More books: I originally had over 20 chapters for this book, and come up with more exciting topics on a near daily basis in conversations with colleagues. Hence, this is Part 1. My vision is to release at least two more versions in the series, one of which I hope to include featured guest writers; contributions from other experts within the Internet industry. Plus, then I can cover new topics that come up since the industry changes like the seasons.

All business (my professional props if that's all you care about)

◦ 10 Years of Internet industry **experience** including

     o Information Architecture

     o Internet Strategy Planning & Analysis

     o Business Analysis

     o Online Marketing Strategy and Management

     o Usability Expertise

     o Interface Design

     o HTML/CSS Programming

     o User Testing

To learn more about me, or request that I speak at an event, reach me online at **shiftingthedrift.com**.

Doodle and note-taking space

Lemme Holla Atchya

Translation for un-hipsters: 'Let Me Holler at You', un-coolly known as Acknowledgements

In no certain order of importance, respect owed, or lack thereof:

My Editors
- Richard G for jumping right in and getting his hands dirty and ensuring this book become what it was meant to be
- David H for being the best employee of all time and the most amazing, passionate Internet expert out there, keep it up! He also cleverly suggested the reference to Meatloaf the singer; it is nice!
- Becca for always loving me and seeing me for my true self; she coined the best description I have ever heard of me, that ***I have the thickest outer shell and softest candy center*** of anyone she has met
- Richard S for always inspiring me, challenging me, and being a constant cheerleader
- Mom and Dad for the obvious (life you idiot), and for always supporting me as long as it makes me happy

My Mentors
- Dad for being an award-winning teacher at work and at home
- Mom for teaching me everything she knows about finance, investing and following your dreams, often saying, "If you truly want it, just do it and it will all work out"
- Coach Tuck for kicking my ass and loving me
- Jodi F for being a smart, successful, strong, hip, funny and un-messable-with woman of great accomplishment
- Gordon for knowing when to quit and do what's true to his heart
- Trish B for taking me under her wing and letting me fly away

My Inspiration

- Ashley, my partner (no I am not gay and yes he is a man, a very hairy Italian one at that) for loving me for me and letting me be me, even when he is the brunt of most of my Internet humor
- Jonathan, my little brother, for living into his destiny as the sensitive and honorable family man; I can't wait to meet my first little nephew this winter!
- Matt, a soul mate, now passed on, for keeping a song in my heart
- Bjorn, another soul mate, also passed, for protecting me
- Gloria Holden, my psychic contributor, for talking straight
- The Red Hot Chili Peppers for constantly bringing their funky blend of in-your-face bass-thumping, heart-pumping freaky-stylings as a backdrop for my life's adventures
- John Higgins, a dear friend I haven't seen in forever, for honing my specific blend of sarcasm, dark humor and love for life
- My dogs for giving me a daily glimpse into what a life full of love, peace and laughter is all about
- Carlo and Rossi and Lay's Potato Chips for providing near constant fuel of Paisano jug wine and the new Lay's Chile Limon flavor chips, which if you haven't yet tried, put it on the list of things you must do before you die. They are the ultimate combination of mild spice, sour lime and salt. I am in love; and in need of some serious working out!

References

About the Internet

- ° livinginternet.com
- ° internet101.org
- ° internetworldstats.com

Blogs and Industry Sites

- ° clickz.com/stats
- ° digital-web.com
- ° sempo.org
- ° alistapart.com
- ° webword.com/wp
- ° kaushik.net/avinash

Books / Further Reading

- ° "Call to Action" by Bryan and Jeffrey Eisenberg
- ° gettingreal.37signals.com
- ° 37signals.com/whitepaper
- ° "Don't Make Me Think" by Steve Krug

Education and Training

- ° adaptivepath.com/events/training
- ° uie.com/events

Information Architecture

- ° iainstitute.org
- ° boxesandarrows.com
- ° jjg.net/ia
- ° edwardtufte.com

Just for Fun
- youcantgetthere.com/iamhere
- subservientchicken.com
- laptop.org
- etsy.com
- webpagesthatsuck.com *(use the checklists)*
- popvssoda.com
- dack.com/web/bullshit.html
- lulu.com *(self-publish your own book)*
- freecsstemplates.org *(free sites)*

Online Best Practices, Inspiration and Award Winners
- welie.com/patterns
- useit.com
- webbyawards.com
- cssbeauty.com
- cssvault.com

Search Marketing and Analytics Tools
- google.com/analytics
- omniture.com
- clicktracks.com
- sempo.org
- kaushik.net/avinash

Research, Benchmarks and Stats

- w3.org
- index.fireclick.com
- internetworldstats.com
- w3schools.com/browsers
- clickz.com/stats
- hitwise.com
- iprospect.com
- jupiterresearch.com
- hoovers.com
- did-it.com
- enquiroresearch.com
- eyetools.com

Testing and Tracking

- google.com/analytics
- omniture.com
- clicktracks.com
- validator.w3.org

Writing for the Web

- useit.com/papers/webwriting
- alistapart.com/articles/writeliving
- websitetips.com/webcontent
- webdesignfromscratch.com/writing_for_the_web.cfm

Visit **youcantgetthere.com/iamhere** to contribute to the blog, watch the videos or get FREE help finding the best firm to help you achieve online success.

www.ingramcontent.com/pod-product-compliance
Lightning Source LLC
Chambersburg PA
CBHW031812190326
41518CB00006B/309